STAR WARS
INSIDER™

ICONS OF THE GALAXY

THE BEST OF *STAR WARS INSIDER*

TITAN

WWW.TITAN-COMICS.COM

Star Wars Insider
Icons of the Galaxy
ISBN: 978-1-78585-1933

Editor Jonathan Wilkins
Senior Executive Editor Divinia Fleary
Copy Editor Simon Hugo
Designer Russell Seal
Art Director Oz Browne
Publishing Manager Darryl Tothill
Publishing Director Chris Teather
Operations Director Leigh Baulch
Executive Director Vivian Cheung
Publisher Nick Landau

Published by Titan
A division of
Titan Publishing Group Ltd.,
144 Southwark Street,
London, SE1 0UP

Collecting material
previously published in
Star Wars Insider magazine.

A CIP catalogue record for this title is available from the British Library.

First Edition November 2017
10 9 8 7 6 5 4 3 2 1

Printed in China.

Acknowledgments
Titan would like to thank the cast and crews of the *Star Wars*
films, and the animated series: *Star Wars: The Clone Wars* and
Star Wars Rebels. A special thanks also to the teams at Dark Horse
Comics, Marvel Comics, and Del Rey for their contributions
to this book. A huge thanks also to Brett Rector, Sammy Holland, and
Michael Siglain at Lucasfilm for all of their invaluable help in putting
this volume together.

ICONS OF THE GALAXY

THE BEST OF *STAR WARS INSIDER*

CONTENTS

GEORGE LUCAS'S ORIGINAL *STAR WARS* REVEALED

THE **STAR WARS** INSIDER

ISSUE 144
U.S. $7.99
CAN $9.99
OCTOBER 2013

TITAN

LEIA
A PRINCESS OF THE PEOPLE

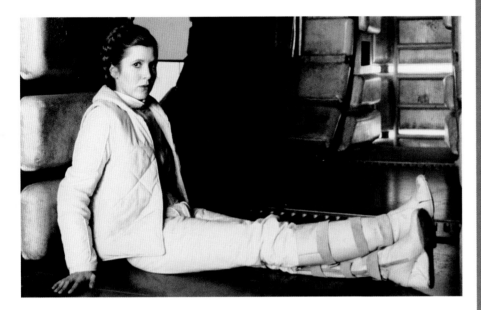

Few characters in motion picture history are as iconic and important as Princess Leia Organa. She's beautiful, of course, and for a large part of *A New Hope* she's waiting to be rescued, but she's no damsel in distress. In fact, to paraphrase Julia Roberts' character in *Pretty Woman*, on being rescued, Leia rescues her rescuers right back.

Quick with a pithy comeback, she's fast to act and defiant in the face of male aggressors, be it Darth Vader, Grand Moff Tarkin or Jabba the Hutt. She's also a strong leader: never mind what *The Empire Strikes Back*'s opening crawl would have you believe, Leia is clearly the leader of the freedom fighters guiding the rebel forces to their vital victories against the Empire.

Ultimately, Leia has been a huge influence. Not only in the *Star Wars* saga, with characters such as Padmé, Rey, and Jyn, but also in popular entertainment across the board, paving the way for stronger female roles.

As an added bonus to our look at the importance of Leia in the *Star Wars* saga, we present a brief, but typically humorous interview with Carrie Fisher.**—Jonathan Wilkins**

Carrie Frances Fisher was born on October 21, 1956 in Burbank, California. Her parents were the actress Debbie Reynolds and singer Eddie Fisher. She made her movie debut in the 1975 movie Shampoo, *alongside Warren Beatty and Julie Christie. This was followed by a diverse series of roles, including work with Woody Allen, Rob Reiner, Sidney Lumet, and David Cronenberg.*

Fisher was also an accomplished writer. Her bestselling novel Postcards from the Edge *was turned into a film, and her autobiographical one-woman play* Wishful Drinking *also became a book. Behind the scenes, she enjoyed a successful career as a script doctor, working on the likes of* Hook *(1991),* Lethal Weapon 3 *(1992),* Sister Act *(1992),* Mr. and Mrs. Smith *(2005).*

Almost 40 years after she first played Princess Leia, Fisher reprised the role for Star Wars: The Force Awakens *and* Star Wars: The Last Jedi *before her untimely death on December 27, 2016.*

LEIA

PRINCESS OF THE PEOPLE

MUCH HAS BEEN WRITTEN ABOUT HOW LUKE SKYWALKER'S JOURNEY FROM FARMBOY TO JEDI HAS INFLUENCED MODERN STORYTELLING. BUT LUKE'S TWIN SISTER HAS ALSO PAVED THE WAY FOR SUBSEQUENT HEROINES TO EMBARK ON THEIR OWN JOURNEYS. TRICIA BARR EXPLORES HOW LEIA INTRODUCED MOVIEGOERS TO A NEW TYPE OF HEROINE.

The influence of mythologist Joseph Campbell, who charted narrative patterns and archetypes across the history of storytelling, on *Star Wars* has been well documented. But while most of the focus has tended to be on Luke Skywalker's "Campbellian" hero's journey, Leia Organa also marked a twist on a narrative archetype. Leia enters the story as a classic princess character—but it soon becomes clear she is no typical fairy tale princess. When scholars look back on the last century of cinema, the influence of *Star Wars'* first heroine will not be forgotten. By the 1970s, barriers were being broken down and the modern feminist movement had gained prominence. Wonder Woman graced the cover of the first *Ms.* magazine. And the *Star Wars* opening crawl introduced a character unlike any princess seen previously: The "custodian of the stolen plans that can save her people and restore freedom to the galaxy."

George Lucas's bold attempt at creating a modern princess needed an actress who could pull it off. While it's true Leia is a lone woman amid a male-dominated cast, she represents what it means to be a woman in a position of power during this era. Given cinnamon rolls for hair, a white drape dress, and a weapon in hand, Carrie Fisher compellingly delivers the film's smart, witty dialogue. In her first on-screen moments, Leia transfers the stolen plans to R2-D2, then engages stormtroopers as a diversion for the droid's escape. She introduced a generation of moviegoers to a new type of female character—one fully empowered to take charge of her destiny.

Dangling the prospect of riches, white knight Luke enlists smuggler Han in the rescue of the space opera's warrior princess. Leia plays her part and dashes out of her cell with her hero—only to realize there wasn't much of an escape plan. Quick thinking and a blaster "borrowed" from her rescuer enable Leia to create an exit opportunity from the detention block. The hero and princess do not get away unscathed from the Death Star: Leia's commitment to the Rebel Alliance results in the destruction of her home planet, while Luke loses his mentor Obi-Wan. She never bends to grief, though, and even consoles Luke. In the end Leia's mission succeeds: Her stolen plans eventually help deliver the rebels' victory.

COMING OF AGE

For *The Empire Strikes Back*, Lucas served as executive producer and writer, and allowed another director, Irvin Kershner, to influence the galaxy far, far away. George Lucas penned the original screenplay, which was polished and improved upon by Lawrence Kasdan, who had already written the script for *The Bodyguard* (later filmed with Whitney Houston)—a story about a "pop princess" in danger. Director Irvin Kershner, meanwhile, envisioned the middle movie of the trilogy as a fairy tale, not science fiction. Leia is the character who carries the emotional weight for the film's second act.

The director and writers of *The Empire Strikes Back* created circumstances for their princess to drop her emotional shields, isolating her from duty to the Rebel Alliance and tying her fate to a scoundrel willing to wear his heart on his sleeve. Over the course of the movie, Leia subtly shifts from the virginal princess, who wears white camouflage appropriate for the ice planet Hoth, to being seen in earthy hues and her tightly-wound braids on Bespin. For a brief moment, Han and Leia are shown interacting in a familiar, unguarded manner—before they are captured by Darth Vader and Leia returns to her white uniform.

In the carbonite chamber, Fisher beautifully conveys the coming-of-age of a young woman who takes an emotional leap of faith and declares her love. While Harrison Ford's ad-lib of "I know" retains Han Solo's cocky swagger, perhaps he didn't need to echo Leia's words because he already had said them. In her 2010 TED Talk entitled The Power of Vulnerability, Brené Brown, a PhD. who has spent a decade studying social interaction, discussed how the courage to be vulnerable is the means to the greatest emotional reward. For an audience familiar with the conceits of fairy tales, *The Empire Strikes Back* counts on the audience's trust that ultimately a happily-ever-after ending would reward the princess who finally dropped her emotional shields.

The 1980s not only ushered in the cinematic shocker of Vader's "No, I am your father," but also such notable blockbusters as *Raiders of the Lost Ark* and *E.T.: The Extra Terrestrial*, which jumpstarted the careers of future Hollywood power-women Kathleen Kennedy and Drew Barrymore. The year after Leia professed her love for Han, Diana Spencer became the Princess of Wales before a global television audience of 750 million. Diana was a princess of the people who championed causes affecting those with fewer advantages in life, such as the victims of AIDS and leprosy, or those ravaged by landmines left behind in the wake of war.

Return of the Jedi opens with an extremely personal quest for Luke and Leia. They step away from the war against the evil Empire to rescue Han from the lair of Jabba the Hutt. Episode VI's first act showcases the teamwork of Lando, Chewbacca, and even the droids. Future storytellers J.J. Abrams and Joss Whedon internalized this collaborative heroism and reflected it years later in their own tales like *Buffy the Vampire Slayer*, *Lost*, *Fringe*, and *Marvel's The Avengers*.

The rescue mission also includes Leia's separation from her male counterparts, when she is forced to don a gold bikini and sit chained to

LEIA INTRODUCED MOVIEGOERS TO A NEW TYPE OF FEMALE CHARACTER.

Jabba's throne. It is impossible to separate the character from the slave Leia attire and its place in the history of storytelling. The visual art of motion pictures emerged along much the same timeline as comics. During the Golden Age of comics, roughly the 1930s-40s, women were often portrayed as career women or superheroines like Wonder Woman. In later years, though, the roles of female characters were increasingly relegated to the superhero's sidekick or romantic interest, and in these secondary roles they were often hyper-sexualized. Slave Leia on the silver screen mirrors Wonder Woman in comics. Neither heroine has clothes to shield them from the male gaze, and Leia wears the chains of slavery much as Wonder Woman's bracelets mark an ever-present reminder of the enslavement of her ancestors. Fisher vividly channels the emotions of a woman using the chains of captivity to slay the grotesque Jabba to gain freedom, and most women who cosplay as slave Leia speak of feeling empowered.

Princess Leia has never quite been embraced by the feminist movement in the way Wonder Woman has, perhaps because of the perception that *Star Wars* was a boys' franchise rather than a pro-feminism vehicle. Yet male storytellers like Abrams and Whedon, who were heavily influenced by *Star Wars*, have made a mark in the entertainment industry with their exceptional female characters.

The remainder of *Return of the Jedi* revisits the warrior princess from Episode IV. Leia volunteers for the combat mission to the forest moon, flies a speeder bike to chase down the biker scouts who might expose the rebels' presence, and mediates with the primitive Ewoks. As her newly revealed twin brother Luke seeks to redeem a father he never knew, Leia and Han assault the shield generator with the help of their Ewok allies. The emotional thematic victory is not just Luke's, as he sees his father return to the light side, but also his sister's. And Han, the poor self-sacrificing scoundrel, finally emerges from his carbonite-induced haze and remembers he already had been given the heroine's heart on Bespin, thus delivering the moment Kershner's fairytale had promised.

Above: A step away from the war against the Empire: Leia 's daring rescue attempt in Jabba's palace.

Opposite page, from top left: Leia onboard the *Millennium Falcon* (ESB); enjoying brief respite on Bespin (ESB); as a member of the Endor strike team (ROTJ).

Main image: Carrie Fisher as the iconic Princess Leia as seen in *A New Hope*.

TRAGIC TURNS

The 1990s continued the trend of modern princesses. Disney's new era of movie heroines began with *The Little Mermaid* and *Beauty and the Beast*, while the *Star Wars* Expanded Universe kicked off with the novel *Heir to the Empire*, continuing the adventures of the Original Trilogy heroes. In over two decades' worth of subsequent Expanded Universe adventures, Leia has faced the prospect of bearing a Skywalker heir burdened by the haunting legacy of the family name, and then the real-life struggle (and guilt) of being a working mother raising children—part of that time serving as the elected Chief of State of a fledgling galactic democracy, no less. Perhaps the Original Trilogy established Leia as a woman capable of withstanding any tragedy almost too well, as the Expanded Universe has seen her endure the death of her youngest son to war, witness her eldest son's plunge to the dark side, and then see his death at the hand of his own twin sister. Amid all the tragic turns, writers like Timothy Zahn and Aaron Allston have managed to create beautifully poignant stories with Leia as a mother figure who is also a warrior princess.

Yoda's dying words, though, took longer to be fulfilled. Leia does not complete her Jedi training until after the New Republic she fought to establish is pulverized by a galactic invasion and her surviving twins Jaina and Jacen Solo have become Jedi Knights. In a rare moment of vulnerability shared with her teenage daughter in the New Jedi Order novel *Rebel Dream*, Leia gives voice to the painful choices at the heart of her own identity: "Sometimes I'm Jedi and sometimes I'm not. Jedi teaching says that you must turn away from fear. But as a politician, I have to experience fear… Sometimes being a Jedi just runs completely counter to your other goals." Leia also reminds her daughter why she continues to fight: "I've had whole *worlds* taken away from me… but not my future." Beyond the movies, Leia finds a way to balance the dueling forces of her heritage, avoiding both the naïve idealism of her politician mother Padmé Amidala and the inability of her Jedi father Anakin Skywalker to master his fear of loss.

Princesses are as visible as ever today. Kate Middleton renewed our fascination with royalty when she married the late Princess Diana's son Prince William. In the TV series *Once Upon a Time*, Snow White is as handy with a bow and arrow as her Prince Charming is with a sword. And *Brave* became the first Disney princess movie to explore the relationship between mother and daughter. Brian Wood's new *Star Wars* comic, meanwhile, features a post-*New Hope* Leia in a story exploring the emotional vulnerabilities of a young woman faced with losing her family, her friends, and her homeworld of Alderaan while also showcasing her capabilities as a warrior and X-wing pilot—to critical and commercial success, including *Star Wars* #1 earning a fourth printing. With an upcoming Original Trilogy-era Leia-centric novel from Martha Wells and the Sequel Trilogy set to embark on new journeys in the galaxy far, far away, it's clear that the impact of *Star Wars*' original heroic princess on storytelling is still unfolding. ☻

Opposite page: Leia enjoys some Endor sunshine in this publicity shot. **Below, clockwise from top left:** In disguise as the mysterious bounty hunter, Boushh; confrontation in Cloud City; raiding the Imperial bunker on Endor.

INTERROGATION DROID!

INSIDER MAKES AN APPOINTMENT WITH *STAR WARS* ROYALTY AS
CARRIE FISHER TELLS IT LIKE IT IS! WORDS: CHRIS SPITALE

Leia's royal title of Princess followed her throughout the galaxy. If Carrie Fisher had a title before her name, what would it be?
Your Royal Holiness.

The title of your memoirs is *Wishful Drinking*—if you were channeling Leia and penning her life story, what would it be called?
What I'm going to call the next book—*The Empire Strikes Wishful Drinking*.

If the strong-willed Padmé Amidala had lived to raise the headstrong Leia, what do you think would have been the dynamic of their mother/daughter relationship?
Well, there would have been a lot of envy—not too dissimilar from my own because it's always unpleasant when your parent is better looking than you are! There would have been a very big rebellion, but hopefully, as a teenager, I'd have made her feel a little less clever.

In *Return of the Jedi*, Leia was clearly in great shape for her summer beach wear. Besides the usual cardio (from always running from the Empire), how do you think she was able to maintain such a lean physique?
There's no time to eat. And everything spills when you make the jump to lightspeed!

If you were playing armchair therapist to the Princess, what kind of advice would you offer?
Get out of space! You know, she's obsessive-compulsive, so take more time for yourself. Go shopping; get a massage! Don't always be in battle; it's just gonna wear you out!

NAME: CARRIE FISHER
ALIAS: PRINCESS LEIA ORGANA

FIRST APPEARANCE:
STAR WARS: EPISODE IV *A NEW HOPE*

Do you think she'd have been a little more easy-going with Han if she were on Prozac?
No, there's just no way you are gonna be easy-going with Han!

If Leia had visited the Mos Eisley cantina, which cocktail would she have preferred?
A smoking mynock!

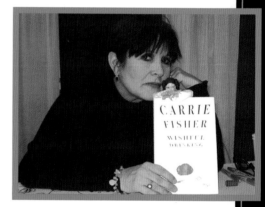

Let's say that after several smoking mynocks Leia decided to karaoke while the cantina band played backup. What song would she select?
Billie Jean (You're Not My Lover).

If you were recasting *Star Wars* today, which actress would you cast in the role of Princess Leia?
Maybe Ellen Page from *Juno*. I also like Mary Louise Parker from *Weeds*. But I don't know if they'd need gaffer's tape.

Since you are a highly-respected script doctor, which *Star Wars* scene would you have liked to have changed?
I would have given myself—as I tried to do—dialogue when I was with Jabba the Hutt. As my co-travelers [Luke, Han and Chewie] are walking away, I wanted to say, "Don't worry about me, I'll be fine... Seriously." ☻

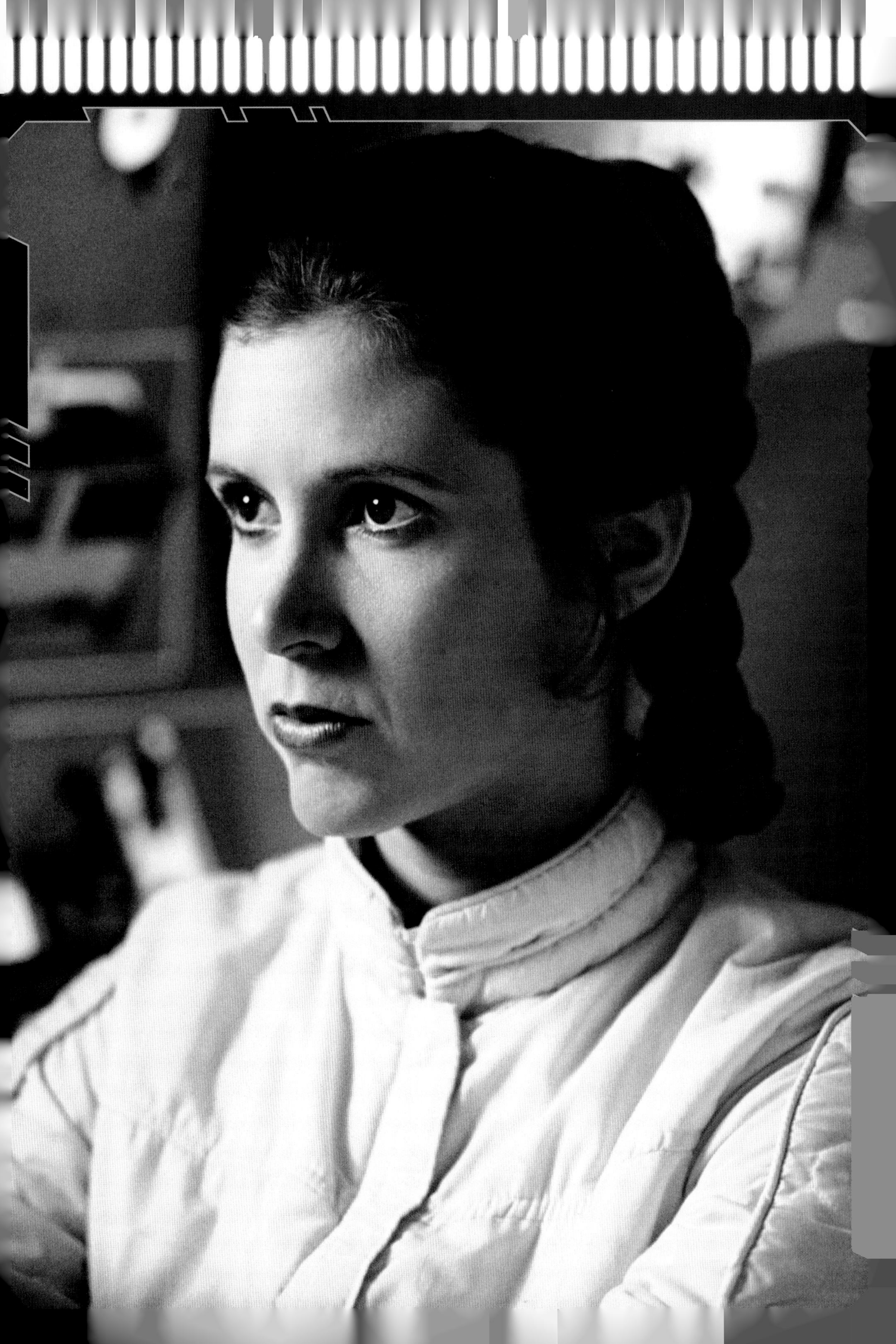

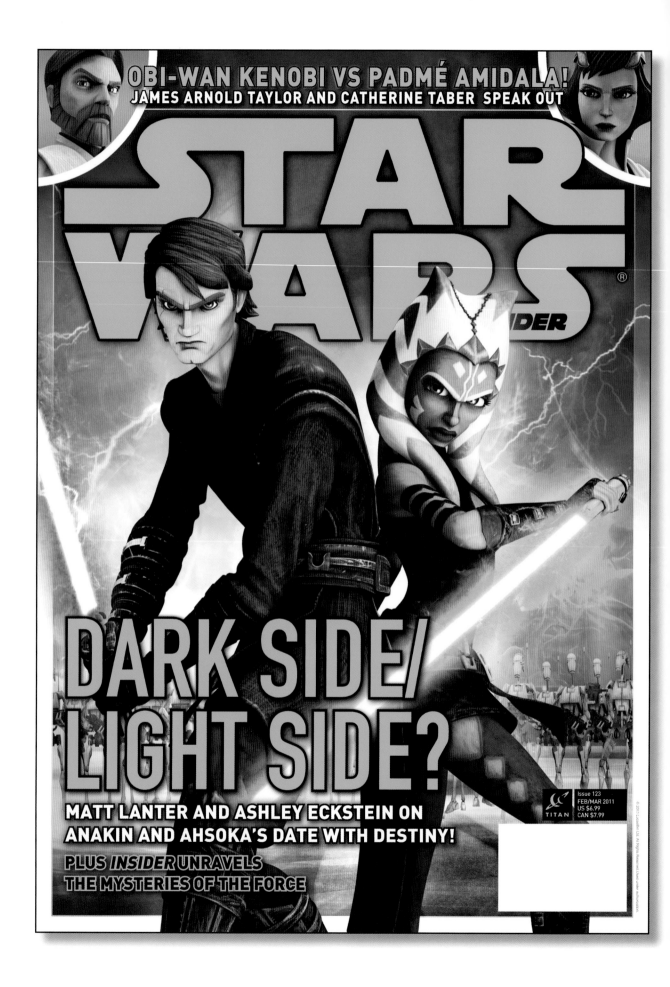

OBI-WAN KENOBI VS PADMÉ AMIDALA!
JAMES ARNOLD TAYLOR AND CATHERINE TABER SPEAK OUT

STAR WARS
INSIDER

DARK SIDE/ LIGHT SIDE?

**MATT LANTER AND ASHLEY ECKSTEIN ON
ANAKIN AND AHSOKA'S DATE WITH DESTINY!**

**PLUS *INSIDER* UNRAVELS
THE MYSTERIES OF THE FORCE**

Issue 123
FEB/MAR 2011
US $6.99
CAN $7.99

COLLECTING
LUKE SKYWALKER

Since the earliest days of *Star Wars'* staggering success, it's been easy to own a part of the saga, thanks to the amazing amount of collectibles produced. But owning all of it? Some really dedicated fans have made a decent stab at it, but it's pretty much impossible!

As the hero of the original trilogy, Luke Skywalker has been well represented in merchandise over the years. Action figures have depicted our hero in all manner of outfits, but serious collecting doesn't stop there. As this feature proves, Luke memorabilia comes in all shapes and sizes. One person's trash is another's highly prized lo-fat Luke Skywalker raspberry yogurt pot!

Dedicated collector Gus Lopez wrote a merchandise column in *Insider* for several years. I used to try to catch him out with very obscure themes: Jabba the Hutt collectibles, Jawas, ice cream, even fast food packaging. I guess Luke was an easy one! I hope you enjoy the treasures Gus—the Indiana Jones of *Star Wars* collecting—has unearthed.—**Jonathan Wilkins**

RETRO WARS

COLLECTING LUKE!

DARTH VADER SPENT A LOT OF TIME SEARCHING FOR LUKE SKYWALKER, BUT COLLECTORS HAVE SPENT EVEN MORE TIME LOOKING FOR MERCHANDISE DEPICTING THEIR HERO.

WORDS AND PICTURES: GUS LOPEZ

There have been over 2,400 unique Luke Skywalker items produced since 1977, giving Luke fans many options to collect their favorite character.

1] Luke was one of the first Kenner action figures offered for pre-order in the Early Bird Certificate kit in 1977. This was followed up in early 1978 with the release of the Luke Skywalker action figure on a 12-back card. The card back featured artwork of Luke's landspeeder (also a Kenner toy) and a detailed close-up of Luke's arm to explain the retracting lightsaber feature.

2] Twenty years later, Icons produced the first ever Luke Skywalker lightsaber replica prop. Made out of a custom machined metal hilt resembling the vintage Graflex camera flash tubes used for Luke's lightsaber prop in the first two films, Icons launched its replica prop line with this popular item. Fans could now own a high quality version of Luke's weapon without needing to hunt down vintage camera equipment.

3] Omni Cosmetics sold Luke Skywalker snowspeeder pilot soap in 1983. It came packaged in a simple window box. The soap was orange to match the pilot uniform colors—just what Luke needed after a smelly night inside the guts of a tauntaun!

1

2

3

"Mallow Bitz" cereal box for its tie-in with the theatrical release.

6] It's hard to imagine that any Luke Skywalker toys considered by Kenner did not make it to market, but several have been documented. For the Micro Collection line, Kenner planned to expand its playsets with a new Dagobah World. This set was to feature a figure of Luke in his X-wing outfit. Early in the design stages for the *Return of the Jedi* line, Kenner considered a version of the Luke Jedi Knight figure with sculpted flowing robes, but this was later changed to a simpler outfit

4] Luke was featured in convention exclusives including Luke-themed badges at *Star Wars* **Celebration IV, V, Europe**, and **Japan**. Luke Skywalker pewter medallions were among the giveaways at the **Celebration IV** and **Europe** collecting panels. These two medallions were based on an image of the vintage Luke Skywalker action figure.

5] Luke was included in the lineup of yogurt cups for the *Return of the Jedi* promotion by Dairy Time in the United Kingdom. Different flavors of yogurt were assigned to each character, and Luke in his X-wing outfit appeared on the low fat raspberry cups. For the *Star Wars* Special Edition films, Nature's Source created a Luke Skywalker themed

with a detachable cloth cape. Years after the vintage line waned, Kenner explored revitalizing *Star Wars* toys with two-inch scale figures including Luke in his pilot uniform, which was mocked up to pitch the concept.

7] The Star Jars cookie jar line from the 1990s was originally planned to cover nearly two dozen different *Star Wars* characters including Luke. Unfortunately this ill-fated line ceased production after the first six jars, never bringing the Skywalker jar to market. Some collectors, however, have managed to get the Luke cookie jar in prototype form. ☺

STAR WARS REBELS **EXCLUSIVE INTERVIEW INSIDE!**

STAR WARS

INSIDER

DRESSED TO KILL

PLUS:
GEORGE LUCAS
CHRIS CLAREMONT
STAR WARS ROLEPLAYING GAMES

**WHY BOBA FETT
IS STILL THE GALAXY'S
GREATEST BOUNTY HUNTER!**

ISSUE 146
JANUARY
2014

TITAN

US $7.99
CAN $7.99

THE MAN IN THE DENTED MASK

BOBA FETT

ISSUE 146

JANUARY 2014

I probably don't need to remind you that Boba Fett is a big deal with *Star Wars* fans. A *very* big deal.

I gave Jason Fry—a stalwart *Star Wars* author and expert—the job of explaining why this bit-part player is so well loved, despite having so few scenes, even less dialogue, and a blink-and-you-miss-it demise.

Of course, Fry came up with the goods, supplying some solid reasons for Fett's enduring popularity, as well as rounding up his greatest moments.—**Jonathan Wilkins**

THE MAN IN THE DENTED
MASK

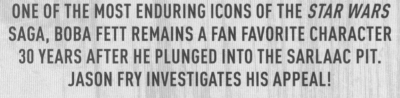

ONE OF THE MOST ENDURING ICONS OF THE *STAR WARS*
SAGA, BOBA FETT REMAINS A FAN FAVORITE CHARACTER
30 YEARS AFTER HE PLUNGED INTO THE SARLAAC PIT.
JASON FRY INVESTIGATES HIS APPEAL!

If you're a *Star Wars* fan of a certain age, you would have been familiar with Boba Fett before you had any idea who he was.

If you were truly lucky, you were at a county fair in San Anselmo, California, and witnessed Fett march in a parade alongside Darth Vader in September 1978—a test run for his prototype costume. If you weren't there, you probably saw him a few weeks later in *The Star Wars Holiday Special*, introduced in a cartoon that was the only watchable part of that debacle. And if you somehow missed that, you undoubtedly sent proof-of-purchases to Kenner the next spring, then waited by the mailbox for your Fett action figure (though he arrived without the spring-loaded rocket pack originally promised).

Kenner told us Fett would play "a major role" in the next *Star Wars* movie, *The Empire Strikes Back*, which strictly speaking wasn't true: Fett did business with Darth Vader, took a shot at Luke Skywalker and abducted Han Solo, but

he had a grand total of four lines and was never referred to by name. Nor was he a major presence in *Return of the Jedi*. Fett's name was finally heard on-screen, but his only line was "What the…,", followed by a dismayed yell after a semi-blind Han accidentally struck his jetpack, sending him hurtling into the Sarlacc pit.

It didn't matter: From these brief minutes of screen time, a *Star Wars* icon had been born. More than three decades later, Fett remains a mainstay of videogames, comics and novels in the Expanded Universe. What accounts for the enduring popularity of this briefly seen, rarely heard bounty hunter? Why is Fett as recognizable as the likes of Darth Vader, Chewbacca and R2-D2, despite far, far less screen time?

The answer—or at least your author's answer—is a combination of visual flair, an evocative character and a certain mystery, one that's lingered despite the growing body of lore about the hunter in the gargoyle helmet.

Art by
Chris Trevas

SINISTER PURPOSE

First of all, there's that costume—a classic design (largely the work of Joe Johnston and Ralph McQuarrie) that practically oozes menace. Fett's armor isn't glossy and pristine, like that of Vader and his stormtroopers—it's battered and dinged, from the scarred helmet and tattered cloak to the pitted breastplate. Every gouge and dent feels like it has a tale to tell, one that begins with "you should see the other guy." Mysterious symbols adorn Fett's armor, a jetpack and missile are strapped to his back, scalps hang over one shoulder, and his arms and legs bristle with weapons and tools of unknown but undoubtedly sinister purpose.

Jeremy Bulloch, who played Fett in *Empire* and *Jedi*, gave the character an air of implacable calm, with the slightest turn of the head conveying danger. There was the deliberate way Fett prepared his starship *Slave I* to pursue the *Millennium Falcon*, the brief glance exchanged with Lando Calrissian as Han is tormented, and his signature moment—his cool, unhurried entrance into Cloud City's dining room behind Vader. In *Jedi*, Fett stood among the thugs in Jabba's throne room, offering Boushh a professional nod, one gunslinger to another. This stillness and sense of purpose made Fett's bursts of action—snapping his rifle up to aim at Chewbacca, or igniting his jetpack to fly from Jabba's sail barge—all the more striking.

But the Fett of *Empire* and *Jedi* wasn't just about looks—he *sounded* deadly, too. When he joined Vader on Cloud City, we heard his spurs clinking. And his voice, as originally supplied by Jason Wingreen, sounded raw and scraped from disuse. Fett, we sensed, was a being of the fewest possible words, surrendering each syllable reluctantly.

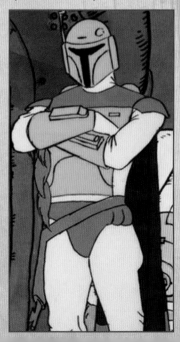

A MYSTERIOUS STRANGER

The mishmash of worn gear, the spurs and the conspicuous weaponry are familiar trappings of an archetype often seen in Westerns: The Mysterious Stranger. Fett belongs to a long lineage of violence-haunted drifters who arrive in peaceful towns, their pasts cloudy and their purpose unknown. Think John Wayne in *The Searchers*, Alan Ladd as Shane, or Clint Eastwood in any number of movies. We don't know who these men are, but we register their travel-worn clothes and their familiarity with a gun, and we know their grim stares promise a reckoning is at hand. But at least these men have faces—in *Empire*, Fett is invisible and unknowable, hidden behind his T-shaped visor.

It's a powerful archetype—and it's this essential mystery that has kept Fett an icon, even as we've learned more than we ever could have dreamed (and perhaps wanted to know) about the character's past.

Fett vanished into the toothed maw of the Sarlacc in *Return of the Jedi*, a rather casual demise for so good a character—and a death the nascent Expanded Universe would soon undo. Marvel Comics wasted no time resurrecting Fett—the Sarlacc spat him out in its very first comic book to hit newsstands after Episode VI, though his escape was brief. In 1991, Dark Horse also brought Fett back in *Dark Empire*, with Han and Leia finding their old nemesis very much alive and determined to collect the price on their heads. Fett even got more screen time, albeit retroactively: The special edition of *A New Hope* digitally added him to the thugs threatening Han in Mos Eisley, while a pickup shot for the revised *Return of the Jedi* saw him stroke a dancer under her chin.

BOBA FETT IS INVISIBLE AND UNKNOWABLE, HIDDEN BEHIND HIS T-SHAPED VISOR.

FETT'S GREATEST HITS...

Seven tales that rank among Boba Fett's most evocative adventures....

"The Last One Standing"—In the 1996 anthology *Tales of the Bounty Hunters*, Daniel Keys Moran portrays Fett as a brutal, stunted man with a chilly, inflexible sense of morality, giving the character complexity without surrendering his mystery. The story ends with a no-longer-young Fett and Han Solo locked in combat, the outcome yet to be determined. Many of the facts in Moran's tale have been overwritten by the prequels, but his elegiac ending remains one of the Expanded Universe's best moments.

"Bounty"—Perhaps the most stylish episode of *The Clone Wars*, this 2012 tale sees Fett leading a crew of hunters – including Dengar, Asajj Ventress and the cooler-than-cool C-21 Highsinger—through the caverns of Quarzite aboard a speeding hover-train. The young hunter is capable enough that we see what he'll become, but still inexperienced enough to need more lessons.

"Twin Engines of Destruction"—Collected in the Dark Horse trade paperback *Bounty Hunters*, this 1997 Andy Mangels tale has art by John Nadeau and Jordi Ensign. Mangels' Fett does a lot while saying little, making every word count. And while Jodo Kast may wear Fett's armor, he's no match for his rival's ruthlessness.

Enemy of the Empire—This 1999 Dark Horse series, written by John Wagner, with art by Ian Gibson, John Nadeau and Jim Amash, is the stuff of fanboy dreams, sending Fett up against Darth Vader himself on a forlorn world. It works: Wagner's Fett is pitiless and resourceful, and the storyline is by turns darkly funny and quietly unsettling.

Death, Lies and Treachery—A 1998 collection from Dark Horse, this trade paperback combines three John Wagner tales illustrated by Cam Kennedy. Fett outwits space pirates, Hutts and other ne'er-do-wells, and even though the character is silent, the artwork conveys Fett as a shrewd professional at the top of his game.

"Boba Fett: Agent of Doom"—This 2000 Dark Horse comic by John Ostrander, with Cam Kennedy art, shows Fett as an agent of good... or at least justice. He pursues the crew of an Imperial death ship for a pittance, determined to remind the galaxy what the name Boba Fett means. (Look for it in the 2007 trade paperback *Boba Fett: Man With a Mission*.)

The Mandalorian Armor—The first book of K.W. Jeter's 1998 trilogy comes gloriously to life when Fett and a gang of hunters, including the unforgettable D'harhan, arrive on the planet Circumtore for a confrontation with the Shell Hutts. Jeter ratchets the tension sky-high before releasing it in a bravura showdown.

THIS IS MY FACE.

BUT WHO IS HE?

Meanwhile, with the Expanded Universe growing to include more and more tales, Fett had gained a back-story. He was born Jaster Mereel, became a Journeyman Protector on the planet Concord Dawn, then was forced into exile and acquired a suit of Mandalorian battle armor and a new identity, becoming the galaxy's most feared bounty hunter. But his face remained a mystery. A 1994 trading card showed a helmetless Fett with white hair, blank white eyes and pointed ears. That was classified as an artist's what-if, but a 1997 comic revealed a human Fett hiding his face behind bandages, his back puckered with Sarlacc scars.

A 1994 TRADING CARD SHOWED A HELMETLESS FETT.

From left, opposite page: The true face of Fett? Art by Jon Nadeau and Jordi Ensign. From *Twin Engines of Destruction* by Andy Mangels; Dan Bereton's speculative take on Fett for a Topps' trading card; Fett with his prize: Han Solo.

Tweets on Fett

We asked *Star Wars* fans on Twitter why they love Boba Fett. Here are some of the best tweets!

It was the same as Maul. They had very few lines and decided that action was louder than words.
@Dareian_Frost

Boba Fett is a classic case of "less is more." Few lines, large screen presence, premature demise.
@Brad_Monastiere

Ruthless. Unscrupulous. Unflinching. Unstoppable. "You can run but you'll only die tired."
@bonejangles13

Who's the cat that won't cop out, when there's danger all about? (Fett) Right on!
@ngematic

The fact I chose him as my 1st costume build for the 501st and I'm a woman! Enough said!
@crazy4bobafett

His backpack's got jets!
@heatmerc

Thanks for your tweets! Don't forget to follow
@star_insider

A NEW HISTORY

Then, in 2002, we had to unlearn everything we had learned. *Attack of the Clones* introduced us to a bounty hunter in familiar though differently colored Mandalorian armor. This was Jango Fett, the template for the Kaminoans' clone army. As part of Jango's compensation, the Kaminoans gave him an unaltered clone of himself – his "son" Boba. We had met a helmetless Boba Fett at last, and he was just a boy, one destined to inherit his father's starship, career and ruthless reputation. Our last sight of Boba was a haunting, instantly iconic image: An orphan in the wreckage of the Geonosis arena, pressing his father's helmet to his forehead.

With Fett's new backstory in place, young-adult novels told of his first attempts at the bounty-hunting trade, while *The Clone Wars* TV show revealed his grim apprenticeship with the assassin Aurra Sing. Storytellers invented new run-ins between Fett and Solo and new missions undertaken for Vader and Jabba the Hutt. We saw Fett become the leader of the Mandalorians, train Jedi, fight the Yuuzhan Vong, and attempt a halting reconciliation with a daughter and granddaughter he and we barely knew. Whatever era they worked in, authors found Fett an irresistible character, and were determined to try their hand at penning new adventures for him. (I'm no exception—*The Essential Guide to Warfare* recounts a tense meeting between Fett and the arachnid information broker Balancesheet.)

And so 35 years after his introduction, Fett has gone from forbidding stranger to familiar face. We're used to seeing him without his helmet and in and out of his armor. Authors have told dozens of his adventures, giving us silent Fetts and chatty ones (silent works better). We know about his youthful doubts and his elderly aches and pains.

Yet for all this, Fett retains his fundamental air of mystery. His tangled back-stories and overwritten histories should be frustrating, but somehow they make him an even more satisfying character. We've seen other Mandalorian hunters mistaken for him, and read about brave and/or foolish people who impersonated him, and in the back of our minds we wonder what we really know. Was he born in a vat on Kamino, or amid the fields of Concord Dawn? Did he begin his bounty-hunting career as a stormtrooper who'd killed his commanding officer, an exiled Journeyman Protector, a Mandalorian supercommando, or a boy seeking to avenge a fallen father?

After seeing the prequels, we may think we know the answers—but then an earlier generation of fans had different answers, and an even earlier one had nothing but blanks to be filled in by their imaginations. The Mysterious Stranger is an archetype as old and rich as storytelling itself, and the question it asks—Who Was That Masked Man?—is more powerful than any answer we're given.

Which brings us back to 1997, and that comic with Fett in bandages. Written by Andy Mangels, it shows Fett doing away with Jodo Kast, an impersonator in Mandalorian armor. When fellow bounty hunter Dengar suggests Fett rarely shows his face because of his Sarlacc scars, Fett turns his helmet in Dengar's direction.

"This is my face," he growls.

That was before we'd heard of Jango Fett, or dared to imagine some connection with the mysterious clones of *Star Wars* prequels yet unseen. Yet despite all the times we've seen Fett's face since then, I think Mangels got it right. ☉

STAR WARS

THE FORCE AWAKENS

WARS

INSIDER

FEATURING

HARRISON FORD
CARRIE FISHER
ANTHONY DANIELS
PETER MAYHEW
DAISY RIDLEY
OSCAR ISAAC
JOHN BOYEGA
LUPITA NYONG'O
ADAM DRIVER
GWENDOLINE CHRISTIE
DOMHNALL GLEESON
J.J. ABRAMS
AND MORE!

TITAN
ISSUE #162
US $7.99
CAN $9.99
JAN 2016

HARRISON FORD
HAN SOLO

ISSUE 162
JANUARY 2016

"Chewie. We're home" That was the line in the trailer for *Star Wars: The Force Awakens* that really got people talking. The gruff, weathered voice of Harrison Ford, reprising the role of Han Solo, even moved Lucasfilm president Kathleen Kennedy to remark, "It really gave you chills."

For many years, the idea that Ford would return to the *Falcon* seemed impossible, but return he did, and this interview—conducted during the whirlwind press tour of *The Force Awakens*—finds the actor in fine form. While Ford has always given his all when it comes to *Star Wars*, his deadpan interview style and world-weary outlook has sometimes been mistaken for a lack of interest, but I don't think that is true at all. His remark that, the *Star Wars* films are "iconic representations of what we know about the complications of our lives," shows a canny appreciation for the underlying themes of George Lucas' work.—**Jonathan Wilkins**

Harrison Ford was born July 13, 1942. His mother, Dorothy, was a homemaker and former radio actress, and his father, Christopher Ford, was an advertising executive and a former actor. His brother, Terence, was born in 1945.

An active member of the Boy Scouts of America, he achieved its second-highest rank, Life Scout, and worked as a counsellor for the Reptile Study merit badge (ironic, given Indiana Jones's notable phobia of snakes). In 1960, Ford graduated from Maine East High School in Illinois. He later attended Ripon College in Wisconsin. It was there that he began attending drama classes in his senior year to get over his shyness, and began to act.

The hardcover novelization of *Star Wars: The Force Awakens* is released

Star Wars: Darth Vader Volume 2 —*Shadows and Secrets* trade paperback released

Star Wars: I Am a Droid released

Star Wars: I Am a Jedi released

Star Wars: I Am a Pilot released

Star Wars 14: Vader Down, Part 5 released

Darth Vader 15: Vader Down, Part 6 released, concluding the six-part *Star Wars: Vader Down* crossover event

Marvel Comics' miniseries *Star Wars: Obi-Wan & Anakin* launched

Star Wars: Lando trade paperback released

Star Wars #15: From the Journals of Old Ben Kenobi released

HARRISON FORD IS
HAN SOLO

AN INSTANT HIT WITH AUDIENCES, HARRISON FORD'S PORTRAYAL AS THE ICE COOL HAN SOLO LED TO A GLITTERING CAREER AS A LEADING MAN IN DIVERSE PROJECTS SUCH AS *BLADE RUNNER*, *WITNESS*, *WORKING GIRL*, *THE FUGITIVE*, AND, OF COURSE, THE *INDIANA JONES* SERIES.

Star Wars Insider: When did you find out that there were going to be new *Star Wars* films?
Harrison Ford: It was a couple years ago, but I didn't see the script until I started getting involved.

Did you need persuading to come back?
I had a degree of self-interest. I was very gratified when I first saw the script and thought there were some amazing ideas; interesting things to do. Then I was very excited for the opportunity to work with J.J. Abrams again, whom I've known for a long time [Ford starred in *Regarding Henry* in 1991 which was written by J.J. Abrams].

You've known Kathleen Kennedy for a long time [working on the *Indiana Jones* films]. Was her involvement part of the attraction?
It's the story; it's the movie that's going to be made. Of course, people are a very important part of the mix and you have relationships with people that are very important. I have a very long and fruitful relationship with Kathy Kennedy, so I was glad to be able to work with her again. I thought it was going to be fun. I knew that it would be in good hands, but that wasn't the only attraction to the project.

What did J.J. Abrams tell you about his vision?
We had discussions about the development of Han and his relationship to other characters in the story. They were very interesting and encouraging conversations. Then there was some work done in respect of the questions I had or input that I had with J.J. Abrams, and I was pleased with that. But I'm a "get on at the beginning and off at the end" kind of guy, so I don't really remember the street signs along the way.

Did you enjoy giving more input?
We all had a certain amount of input once we got started. Over the course of making the *Star Wars* films, we worked with three different directors and each of them had a different style and different attitude towards the process. I would say that the relationship with those three different directors was different, but I always felt that there was a degree of collaboration that was comfortable for everybody involved.

What does J.J. Abrams bring to the table as a director?
He's very thoughtful and very wise about human nature and the development of character and relationships. He brings a real sincerity and emotional

understanding to relationships, which is something I was very pleased to see. He's an enormously skilled filmmaker and a very efficient director and producer. So it has been a real pleasure to work with him and all of the members of his team as this film has gone on.

What was that like walking back onto the _Millennium Falcon_ set.
I spent a lot of years here, so it was fun to see it again. I didn't remember it as well as I thought I did. There are things I remember about the cockpit and the funny stuff we went through. On the original cockpit, I asked George to let us get into it, so we could try it on for size. Finally, we did get a chance, Chewbacca [Peter Mayhew] and I, to walk into the cockpit. Of course, he couldn't get into the seat! Flying it developed a little bit between iterations of the first three films, but it started to come back to me. It was fun.

What about working with screenwriter Lawrence Kasdan?
Larry Kasdan has brought a lot of really fantastic opportunities to the character. And, he's been working with J.J. Abrams on the script for a long time. He continued to be with us on the set and came up with some great stuff. I'm happy we had Larry.

What is it like working with newcomers Daisy Ridley and John Boyega?
They are both very engaging personalities; both in their real lives and in their screen characters. I think the audiences will be

---

"FLYING THE _MILLENNIUM FALCON_ DEVELOPED A LITTLE BIT BETWEEN ITERATIONS OF THE FIRST THREE FILMS, BUT IT STARTED TO COME BACK TO ME. IT WAS FUN."

JOHN BOYEGA ON WORKING WITH HARRISON FORD

"As he works on set, he has a great understanding of the artistic side of shooting a movie as well as the technical side of shooting a film. If anyone asks me what I have learned from working with Harrison Ford on _Star Wars_, I've learned that whatever film I go on to after this, shooting a film or a movie as an actor is a balance of the technical and the artistic. As an artist, you're portraying a role, being an actor, and performing. But the camera is the eye of the audience, so you have to also facilitate that. You have to facilitate the lighting, the positions, and the visual effects. Harrison knows how to do all of that with great balance, but also have fun and make it a comfortable set. He hangs out with us after filming. I took him to South East London to a nice Nigerian restaurant. He spoke to me about all the things that he'd been through and all the things he'd seen over the years as an actor. It was great to learn from an actor [like him]. He's a cool man."

"Chewie, we're home"

Instantly iconic, the sight of Han Solo and Chewbacca onboard the *Millennium Falcon* at the close of the first full trailer for *Star Wars: The Force Awakens* brought a lump to the throats and tears to the eyes of audiences around the world.

LAWRENCE KASDAN
"We were very pleased when we wrote that scene. There were so many moments in writing, and it took months and months of J.J. and I alone walking, talking, sitting, and writing. But we did it with a lot of walking around cities; Los Angeles, New York, Paris, and London. I've never written a movie that way. We were talking and recording, and then we'd go someplace and write it down. It was so much more fun than normal writing. We were sitting at a café in Paris, one of the famous cafés where Ernest Hemingway sat, writing *Star Wars*, with J.J.'s computer on the table. We wrote a lot of it walking around Santa Monica, ending up at the Palisades looking at the Pacific Ocean on a gorgeous day. We were doing all the difficult work of story construction, but we did it in incredibly pleasant circumstances. Once it was freezing cold, walking around Central Park. It was a heavenly experience."

KATHLEEN KENNEDY
"It was amazing for everybody. I was sitting by the monitors, near the door of the *Millennium Falcon*, and I turned around and there must have been 150 people from the crew who had all quietly gathered to get around the monitors and see that moment. It was very emotional. Everyone was feeling something slightly historic was going on. It really gave you chills."

LUPITA NYONG'O ON HARRISON FORD

"Working with Harrison has been precious. He knows this stuff. He's worked on this scale of film many times before. He has shorthand with J.J. and the crew. To see him have such control, and yet be so playful. That's been so fascinating. On such a big set, with so many moving pieces, it's easy to get overwhelmed and not know what's going on. But, Harrison always seems to know what's going on and zeroes in on that."

delighted to make their acquaintance and follow them through the story. They're both very inventive and spirited presences. Their characters are very interesting and go through some changes. The casting has been brilliant, in both cases.

Are relatable characters important?
The genius of *Star Wars* has always been this science fiction, fantasy context but underpinned by an emotionally recognizable human story that we all relate to by degree. We all recognize the power of these relationships, and the complications in people's lives, and it's made these films so important to pass on from generation to generation. You can call them family films, but they are iconic representations of what we know about the complications of our lives.

What do you hope audiences will take away from this film?
Recognition of our common humanity and that all of us face the same kinds of problems in our lives, and that there's hope. There's joy in the celebration of right and wrong, and in the recognition of truth that sustains us. And, they'll have fun along the way.

STAR WARS REBELS: LATEST NEWS REVEALED INSIDE!

STAR WARS

INSIDER

PHOTO EXCLUSIVE!
Amazing shots from the *Star Wars* prequels unearthed!

TROOPERS!

EVERYTHING YOU WANTED TO KNOW ABOUT THE EMPIRE'S LOYAL SOLDIERS, INSIDE!

ISSUE 148
APRIL 2014
U.S. $7.99
Can $9.99

TITAN

IMPERIAL ICONS
STORMTROOPERS

ISSUE 148
APRIL 2014

Putting paid to the idea that bad guys only wear black (there's only room for one Dark Lord here!) the Imperial stormtroopers are the white-clad warriors that became instant icons.

Inspiring a group of very worthy fans to dress up as their heroes in aid of charity, the Empire's troops come in a variety of flavors including snowtroopers, scout troopers, and shoretroopers. Many more styles feature in spin-off books, comics, and videogames.

Despite the fact that stormtroopers are often lousy shots and, on more than one occasion, easily outwitted, they continue to be an essential part of *Star Wars* mythology.

In this feature from 2014, Jason Fry takes a detailed look at the stormtroopers of the saga up to that point. Since then, of course, the First Order has risen, so there is probably scope for an all-new article on the subject. Keep an eye on regular issues of *Star Wars Insider* for that one!—**Jonathan Wilkins**

IMPERIAL ICONS

STORMTROOPERS AREN'T JUST GRUNTS, BUT ICONS OF THE *STAR WARS* GALAXY. *INSIDER* INVESTIGATES THE POWER BEHIND THE EMPIRE.
WORDS: JASON FRY

Sometimes the bad guys wear white.

In 1977, audiences had barely recovered from their first jaw-dropping look at an Imperial Star Destroyer when the action switched to inside Princess Leia's captured starship. Joined by the black-armored Darth Vader, white-armored troops with blasters moved quickly and capably down the ship's hallways, killing or capturing her crew and rounding up its passengers. Almost instantly, the *Star Wars* franchise had an iconic villain: The stormtrooper.

In a galaxy designed to look weather-beaten and lived-in, stormtroopers were the exception, identical in gleaming armor. Their helmets resembled skulls, with the subtly disturbing alteration of the mouth grilles from grins to frowns. We never saw their faces, and their electronically filtered voices were all the same. Granted, stormtroopers didn't seem to be great shots, particularly when chasing our heroes. (One even bumped his head.) But as moviegoers, we forgave this bit of storytelling license—and saw that against lesser foes the stormtroopers were coldly efficient shock troops. Any lack of marksmanship was more than made up for by their numbers: Stormtroopers were everywhere aboard the Death Star, or pouring into Mos Eisley and Cloud City, or invading Hoth and Endor.

The classic trilogy was only the beginning. The Expanded Universe of *Star Wars* lore gave us many more stormtrooper variants, took us inside basic training and showed us the men (and women) beneath the helmets. In the real world, thousands of children wore stormtrooper masks with elastic bands for Halloween—and some of them grew up to become adults whose realistic armor would draw "oohs" and "ahhs" at conventions. The prequel trilogy arrived, showing us the stormtroopers' clone forerunners and giving us new insight into their origins. And soon *Star Wars Rebels* will return to a time when stormtroopers were feared, omnipresent foes.

Join the *Insider* for a look at these Imperial servants—from notable units and individuals to their greatest moments on—and off-screen.

THE FIRST TIME...

SOME IDEAS ABOUT STORMTROOPERS DATE BACK FURTHER THAN YOU MIGHT THINK... OR TOOK LONGER TO BEAR FRUIT.

CLONES

Star Wars fans first heard of the Clone Wars in *A New Hope*, but it wasn't until *Attack of the Clones* that we saw Kamino's secret clone army—the forerunners of the stormtroopers. Before Episode II, *Star Wars* lore generally depicted stormtroopers as recruits or conscripts; afterward, it explored the idea that capable or merely influential Imperials were selected for cloning, with Hasbro's stormtrooper action figures even gaining clone faces beneath their helmets. But the idea wasn't new: 1978's *Star Wars Official Poster Monthly* was the first source to say many stormtroopers were clones. Still, perhaps the Expanded Universe was closer to the mark: *Rebels* draws on George Lucas's notes that stormtroopers are recruits, so fervent in support of the Empire that their ideals are actually more uniform than lab-grown troops.

ROBOTS

Star Wars fans of a certain age will no doubt remember patiently explaining to clueless grown-ups that stormtroopers were people in armor, while *Battlestar Galactica*'s Cylons were robots. Still, the idea of droid stormtroopers is a tough one to keep down: *Star Wars* videogames have given us clone troopers cruelly remade as cyborg Phase Zero dark troopers, Hazard troopers with cybernetic limbs and, most famously, the intimidating Dark Troopers from 1995's iconic game, Dark Forces.

ALIENS

The novels *Darksaber* and *Survivor's Quest* introduced stormtrooper ranks that included non-humans. But 1981's *Star Wars* #53 included enormous alien stormtroopers (in oversized armor). They kidnapped Princess Leia and Aron Peacebringer as part of a story that's odd even by Marvel standards, re-using art left over from the cancelled series *John Carter, Warlord of Mars*.

WOMEN

Legacy's Jes Gistang and *The Essential Guide to Warfare*'s Isila Drutch are the best-known members of the rarely explored ranks of female stormtroopers. But this idea is also an old one: In background material prepared for *A New Hope* licensees, Lucas explained that female stormtroopers were rarities aboard the Death Star, but numerous in other units.

NOTABLE STORMTROOPER UNITS

IN THE MOVIES, STORMTROOPERS ARE STORMTROOPERS. BUT THE EXPANDED UNIVERSE HAS GIVEN US SOME NOTABLE UNITS WITH PROUD TRADITIONS:

THE HAND OF JUDGMENT

The five stormtroopers of this rogue unit began as deserters, fleeing the Star Destroyer *Reprisal* after killing a corrupt major in the Imperial Security Bureau. They wound up as unlikely allies of Luke Skywalker and Han Solo, then of the Imperial agent Mara Jade, and finally of Thrawn.

STORM COMMANDOS

The Expanded Universe is a little contradictory about whether the Storm Commandos are a formal unit or a larger subset of stormtroopers. (One strain of lore says General Madine created them before he joined the Rebels.) Notable for their black scout armor and ruthlessness, Storm Commandos are feared insurgents and irregulars.

FAMOUS STORMTROOPERS

WITH THE EXCEPTION OF A BIT OF GOSSIP BETWEEN TROOPS GUARDING THE DEATH STAR'S TRACTOR-BEAM INFRASTRUCTURE, THE MOVIES' STORMTROOPERS ARE ANONYMOUS. BUT THERE ARE PEOPLE BEHIND THE "BUCKETS." MEET FOUR FAMOUS ONES:

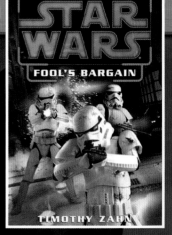

DAVIN FELTH

Onscreen he's the sandtrooper who plucks a bit of plating from the Tatooine sand, exclaiming "Look, sir—droids!" A 1995 short story expanded Felth's biography, making him into the Zelig of the *Star Wars* galaxy: He warned General Veers that enemies could trip up AT-ATs, found the droids' escape pod on Tatooine, and searched the Mos Eisley cantina. The Empire's conduct on Tatooine weighed heavily on Felth, and at Docking Bay 94 he shot his commanding officer in the back, allowing the *Millennium Falcon* to escape. Huh? Sounds like Rebel Alliance propaganda to us!

SU-MIL

A reptilian Eickarie from Kariek, he joined the Empire of the Hand after helping Unit Aurek-Seven liberate his planet. Su-mil earned his stormtrooper commission, reflecting the Empire of the Hand's inclusive views on non-humans, and quickly rose to squad leader. He then fought the Vagaari in the Battle of the Redoubt.

JOKER SQUAD

This unit served the new Sith Empire that rose generations after Luke Skywalker. The squad—later immortalized as a set of action figures—has a little bit of everything, including a tough, grizzled leader (Sergeant Ran "Hardcase" Harkas), a mysterious Mandalorian conscript (Hondo Karr), and a hard-bitten Corellian woman (Jes Gistang).

THE 501st LEGION

The most famous stormtrooper unit, the 501st began as a clone-trooper battalion and was personally assigned to Darth Vader after the rise of the Empire. "Vader's Fist" was disbanded after the Battle of Endor, but the 501st rose again when Thrawn re-created the unit for the Empire of the Hand, and was still around a century later.

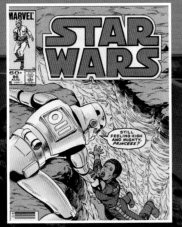

THE TROOPER FROM ALDERAAN

He never gets a name in Marvel's *Star Wars* #86, but his actions are memorable. A former servant to the Organa family, he joined the Empire and captured Princess Leia on Yinchorr. When his commanding officer decided to execute the rebel leader, the trooper sacrificed his own life to save hers. This 1984 tale was written by Randy Stradley, now Dark Horse's vice president of publishing, and marked his *Star Wars* debut.

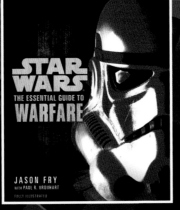

ISILA DRUTCH

Yes, the Empire has female stormtroopers. The best guide to their lives comes from Isila Drutch in *The Essential Guide to Warfare*, who explains that many civilians have probably been a meter from a female stormtrooper and never known it: The armor hides all.

REAL WORLD

No discussion of stormtroopers would be complete without a salute to the men and women of the real-life 501st Legion. Begun by Albin Johnson in South Carolina in 1997, the costuming organization has grown into a worldwide phenomenon, with more than 6,000 members in more than 50 countries. The 501st is a mainstay at conventions and *Star Wars* events, and noted for its extensive charitable work. In 2004, with Lucasfilm's approval, author Timothy Zahn included the 501st in the novel *Survivor's Quest*, making the legion an official part of *Star Wars* lore.

FAVORITE VARIANTS

THE MOVIES SHOW US THREE VARIANT STORMTROOPERS—EPISODE IV'S SANDTROOPERS, EPISODE V'S SNOWTROOPERS, AND EPISODE VI'S SCOUT TROOPERS. (PURISTS MAY ARGUE THAT THE STORMTROOPERS OUTSIDE THE DEATH STAR DOCKING BAY IN EPISODE IV COUNT AS A FOURTH.) COMICS AND VIDEOGAMES HAVE SUPPLIED MANY MORE, AND WHILE SOME OF THEM DON'T SEEM QUITE ESSENTIAL—SWAMPTROOPERS, REALLY?—OTHERS ARE PRETTY COOL.

HERE ARE FIVE FAVORITES:

SHADOWTROOPERS

Stormtroopers in black armor? It's a simple idea and an old one, first introduced by Russ Manning in the 1979 newspaper strip "Gambler's World." But simple works—black-armored troopers look amazing, and are guaranteed to stop traffic at cons.

EMPEROR'S ROYAL GUARD (FIELD ARMOR)

We'll see your black armor and raise you red gear. Well, maybe: The Expanded Universe explains that members of the prestigious Royal Guard stay sharp by rotating anonymously into stormtrooper units. Cool, but even cooler is the rumor that Guardsmen sometimes fight wearing crimson stormtrooper armor.

BEACH TROOPER

What do stormtroopers do for R&R? Well, if you believe LEGO *Star Wars* II: The Original Trilogy, they don Speedos and hit the hot tub—with their helmets on. Canon? Probably not. Hilarious? Definitely.

IMPERIAL NAVY COMMANDO

Imperial Navy Commandos are a mash-up of armor pieces from the classic trilogy, combining a slightly altered stormtrooper helmet with snowtrooper chest armor and the stripped-down look of a scout trooper. Kudos to the Force Unleashed team for an eye-catching design that deserves more attention!

TERROR TROOPER

Combining General Grievous's faceplate with biker-scout duds and taloned gloves doesn't sound like a winner, but it yielded a design worthy of the name, and one of the best parts of The Force Unleashed II.

"IT'S THEM! BLAST THEM!"

FOUR GREAT MOVIE MOMENTS...

THE TAKING OF THE *TANTIVE IV*

In the opening moments of *A New Hope*, Darth Vader's stormtroopers burn through the hatch of Princess Leia's ship and methodically mow down her defenders. Fans love to poke fun at stormtroopers' questionable marksmanship in other scenes, but here they're chillingly accurate.

RAIDING MOS EISLEY

Although the Force helps Obi-Wan and Luke evade the stormtroopers on the outskirts of Mos Eisley, the Imperials are still hot on their tail, thanks to a particularly nosey spy! As the *Millennium Falcon* readies for takeoff, the troops march through the streets, scattering Tatooine citizens before them. A showdown at Docking Bay 94 awaits...

"IMPERIAL TROOPS HAVE ENTERED THE BASE!"

In *The Empire Strikes Back*, Princess Leia refuses to leave Hoth's command base until all personnel have evacuated. Only an ominous message convinces her it's time to go—a staticky warning, almost instantly cut off, that "Imperial troops have entered the base!" Moments later we see the stormtroopers (in their cold-weather gear) racing through the corridors on a search-and-destroy mission. Striding in their midst: Lord Vader himself.

ORDER 66: CORUSCANT

In one of the greatest shots from *Revenge of the Sith*, a cloaked Anakin Skywalker leads clone troopers up the stairs of the Jedi Temple. Okay, the Republic hasn't fallen yet. But Anakin has become Darth Vader, many of the clones he's leading will serve as stormtroopers, and the Jedi Order's extinction is at hand. Welcome to the dark times.

...AND THREE FROM THE EXPANDED UNIVERSE

HUMAN AFTER ALL

In the 1994 novel *Jedi Search*, the New Republic's Mon Mothma conducts fruitless peace talks with the Empire's Furgan. The two engage in a diplomatic tussle over whether Furgan can bring his stormtrooper bodyguards, which Mothma settles in an ingenious way: The troops must remove their helmets. Underneath—and no longer anonymous— are some young cadets.

...OR PERHAPS NOT

The novel *Survivor's Quest* made the 501st Legion canon in 2004, but the real treat for stormtrooper fans was the e-book *Fool's Bargain*, in which a squad from the 501st strikes an uneasy bargain with an alien tribesman, Su-mil, to fight a warlord. This isn't Palpatine's Empire: At the end Su-mil is invited to join the 501st.

A FAMILY SQUABBLE

The 2005 videogame Battlefront II gave us a scenario no *Star Wars* fan could resist. Fearful of the Empire's growing power, rogue Kaminoans create a new force of clone troopers from Jango Fett's DNA. Sent to eliminate this threat are stormtroopers from the 501st, led by Boba Fett. (Who, of course, is an unaltered clone of Jango.) Stormtroopers vs. clone troopers, fighting for control of their birthplace? Sign us up!

EXPANDED

Jason Fry has authored many *Star Wars* books including *The Essential Guide to Warfare* and *Star Wars: The Clone Wars: Episode Guide*. Follow him on Twitter at @jasoncfry

UNIVERSE

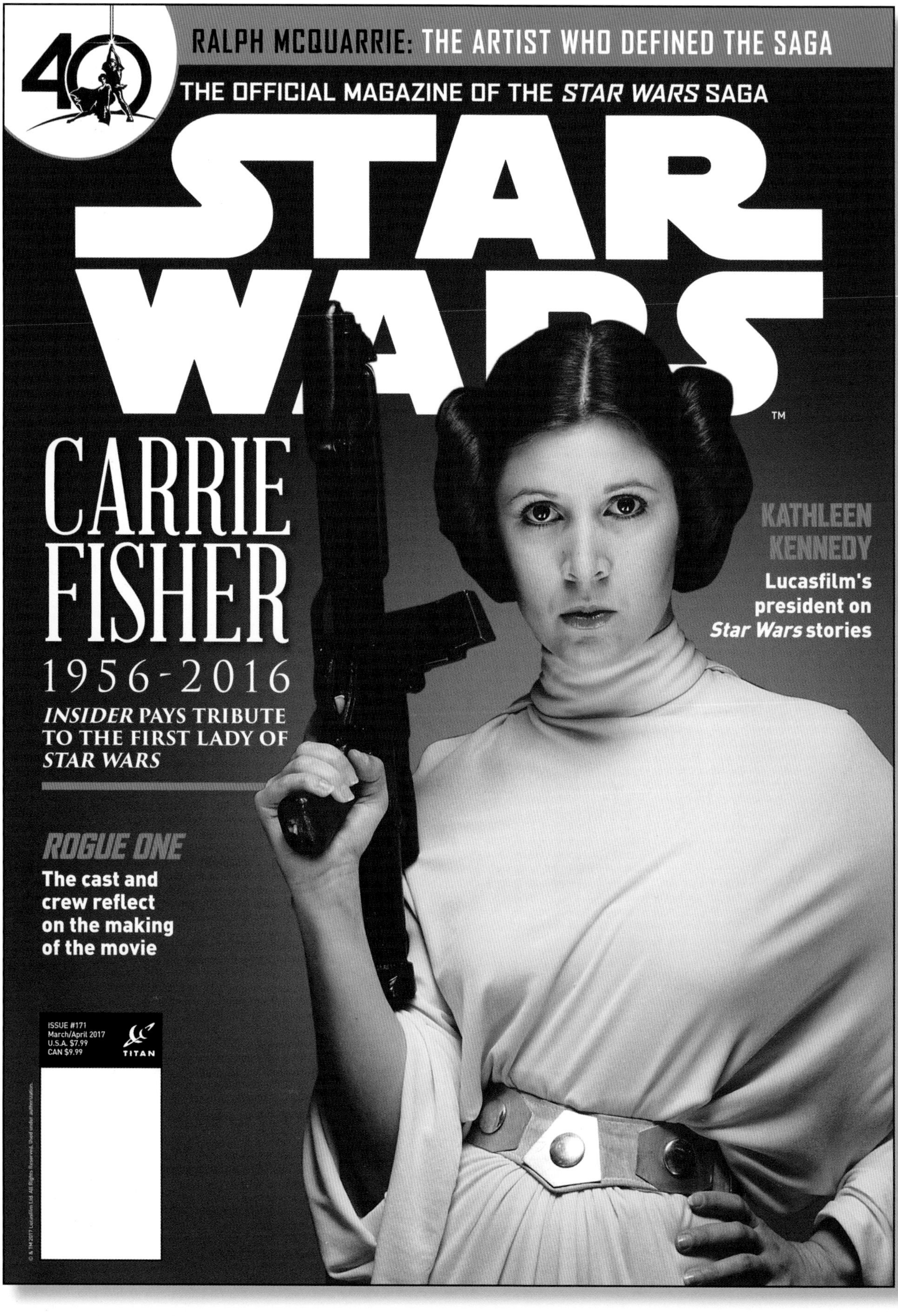

40
RALPH MCQUARRIE: THE ARTIST WHO DEFINED THE SAGA
THE OFFICIAL MAGAZINE OF THE STAR WARS SAGA
STAR WARS
TM
CARRIE FISHER
1956-2016
INSIDER PAYS TRIBUTE TO THE FIRST LADY OF STAR WARS
KATHLEEN KENNEDY
Lucasfilm's president on Star Wars stories
ROGUE ONE
The cast and crew reflect on the making of the movie
ISSUE #171
March/April 2017
U.S.A. $7.99
CAN $9.99
TITAN

BEN MENDELSOHN
DIRECTOR ORSON KRENNIC

ISSUE 171
MAR/APR 2017

An instant icon, Orson Krennic's distinctive look was popular with fans long before *Rogue One: A Star Wars Story* was released in December 2016. In fact, the caped villain was a popular cosplay choice at the *Star Wars* Celebration convention held in London during the previous summer. One of those cosplayers was Ben Mendelsohn, the actor who actually plays Krennic, who attended the *Rogue One* panel in full costume, and full character!

Given that *Star Wars* has delivered some truly memorable bad guys over the years, it says a lot that Ben Mendelsohn was able to craft a character who could stand toe to toe with Grand Moff Tarkin and Darth Vader and hold his own.—**Jonathan Wilkins**

Paul Benjamin Mendelsohn was born on April 3, 1969 in Melbourne, Australia. Following early success as a TV actor, he garnered critical acclaim on the big screen in The Year My Voice Broke *(1987), for which he won the Australian Film Institute Award for Best Supporting Actor. Roles in* The Big Steal *(1990),* Spotswood *(1992),* The New World *(2005),* Australia *(2008) and* The Dark Knight Rises *(2012) followed.*

"YOU CAN'T HAVE A BAD DAY AT WORK WHEN YOU LOOK UP AND YOU SEE THERE ARE STORMTROOPERS AROUND."

BEN MENDELSOHN

SUAVE AND SINISTER, DIRECTOR ORSON KRENNIC PROVED TO BE A WORTHY VILLAIN, STANDING SHOULDER-TO-SHOULDER WITH SOME OF THE GREATS OF THE FRANCHISE. ACCOMPLISHED ACTOR BEN MENDELSOHN SHARES HIS THOUGHTS ON PLAYING A BAD GUY AND BEING SADISTIC ON SET!

The impressive sight of Director Krennic flanked by his loyal Death Troopers.

Star Wars Insider: Can you tell us how you were introduced to the role and what your initial reaction was?
Ben Mendelsohn: I was asked to go and meet Gareth Edwards, our director, and I knew it was something to do with _Star Wars_. So, that was pretty exciting right there. He basically told me as much as he could about who this guy was and where he fit into the scheme of things. Then it became something I was fortunate enough to get to do.

How did you feel about stepping in as a _Star Wars_ villain?
I didn't quite know how that was going to form up, but I felt okay about it. The thing is, when you have Darth Vader on the playing field, you don't have to worry, because no one's taking Vader's spot. Darth Vader is one of the great all-time movie villains there will ever be. So, you don't have to really stress out about it. No one's topping Vader, so you can relax and just do what you're there to do because you have Vader, and when you have Vader, things go okay.

How did Gareth Edwards describe Krennic to you?
Gareth described Krennic to me as a guy who didn't come up through the officer class, if you like; he was more of a guy from the outer colonies who had made his way up more by virtue of the way he'd

"KRENNIC SEES THE EMPIRE AS MAINTAINING ORDER AND THAT IT IS ESSENTIALLY CORRECT IN WHAT IT DOES."

conducted himself, and by his abilities. So, Krennic's voice is not ever meant to be the pure officer-class voice that you associate with the _Star Wars_ universe. But Krennic is very driven about the Death Star project. Gareth laid out Krennic's situation for me, with a rundown of the story, but left it loose enough that things would form up.

Why is Krennic so consumed with the creation of the Death Star?
It's very simple why Krennic is so devoted to it. The politics that go on at the heart of the _Star Wars_ story are crucially important to the way the story plays out. As an audience, we don't necessarily know too much about it. We know that there's an Imperial Senate and we know that having control of that Senate, or the Emperor being able to work with that Senate, is crucially important. So, an unwieldy Senate or a negative Senate is a constant danger to the way the political system works. If you have the Death Star, you, in

effect, can circumvent any problems that might occur within the Senate, because you all of a sudden bring overwhelming force to bear, basically, because the Death Star can take out an entire planet. There is nothing that comes even close to that kind of ability at the time. So, that's why it's so important. Essentially, the Emperor realizes what a good thing this would be to have, what a significant strategic asset it would be, and Krennic believes that he can oversee and implement this project, which in fact he can.

Was it fun to play the sadistic side of the character?
You can't have a bad day at work when you look up and you see there are stormtroopers around. There's no more fun to be had, really, in terms of the type of stuff you do than this.

Do you feel like Krennic is searching for a sense of belonging in some way?
No, I don't think of Krennic so much in those terms. Inside an Imperial Court strange things can happen. Who knows what would happen if the Emperor were to depart and there was a power vacuum? I think Krennic is someone going about his work. I think he sees the Empire as maintaining order and that the Empire is essentially correct in what it does. I think Krennic's going to work hard to make sure that it stays that way. As for what he's

Ben Mendelsohn as
Director Orson Krennic.

Krennic confronts Galen Erso, on the remote world of Lah'mu

working toward, well, I think we can just assume that power is something that has its rewards. I think that if you're positioned well enough inside the upper echelons of the Empire, you have a lot of power.

Krennic uses quite brutal tactics. Do you think he's ever torn about his use of force?
I am sure that Krennic, all things being equal, would rather people were sensible and just realized that if one turns up with six death troopers and says, "We're going to go now," that would be the end of the story. When it's not, at that point it just becomes the responsibility of the other people. I don't think it's a case of Krennic's brutal tactics. I think it's a "fait accompli" when Krennic turns up with a ship and six death troopers and says, "You've been very hard to find. I need you. We need you. The project needs you. Do the right thing." You just come. Because one way or another, you're coming.

What do you think of the look of the Empire?
These sets look really beautiful. There's a real beauty about the way the Empire looks, and a great depth to the darkness of the Empire.

Can you talk about the director, Gareth Edwards, as a person and his style?
I think the great thing about Gareth, and there are many great things, is that first

and foremost, Gareth's a fan. Gareth is a huge fan of *Star Wars*. No one's happier to be making this film than Gareth Edwards. He is the happiest man among us. It just means so much to him. Gareth's able to do incredible and really beautiful work with his visuals and his effects stuff. He's brilliant at it. But he's very collaborative too. He wants people's full engagement. Gareth is not someone who is going to ever talk down to someone that he works with in any way. And Gareth will find a way to draw out what he needs from any particular person. Gareth's also incredibly hands-on. This is a guy who will shoot a lot of the day himself, in terms of the camera and whatnot. Gareth's got a big job. I wouldn't even start to know how to do what he does.

Do you feel that more focus is being placed on the intricacies of the characters and their relationships in this film?
I think that one of Gareth's great strengths is that he really does see characters from all sides. He can take Krennic's position and make sense of the world the way Krennic might see it. When he was talking to us and when he was directing us, he was able to take a lot of viewpoints into being. It seemed pretty apparent that he's very interested in the interplay between the characters and the fullness of them. *Star Wars* has very clean archetypes and I think Gareth hopes in this film to fill some things

out. There are a lot of thoughts from different characters about what needs to be done and how it should be done. That is all to do with the Death Star. For one side it needs to be built, and it needs to be built successfully. For another side, it must be destroyed at all costs. And the how and why it's all done is very important. So, I think Gareth has made a very full, rounded bunch of characters within lines that still remained clean.

Did you try to stay grounded with the characters despite the grandeur of the world they inhabit?
I think we did. The real thing about it is being able to express feelings and vibes within the words and also the other things that you're telling about the story and the universe. What the original *Star Wars* says and what it's about is really beautiful. Where they take that lore from *A New Hope* and *The Empire Strikes Back* and what Luke goes through and the influences on Luke, sets a template for everything that follows. Jyn's heroic journey is different than Luke's, but she's still got some of the same decisions to make. In a lot of ways she faces odds that are much tougher than Luke's. In some ways the decisions that she has to make are much more difficult decisions than Luke's were. In a lot of ways they have more impact if she gets it wrong. ☙

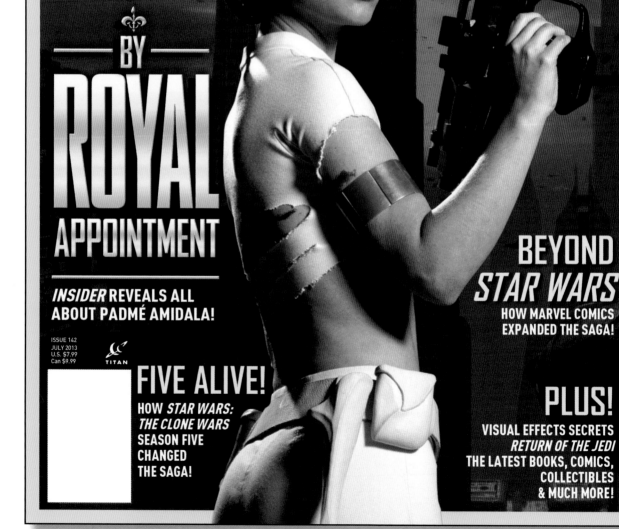

STAR WARS

INSIDER®

BY ROYAL APPOINTMENT

INSIDER REVEALS ALL ABOUT PADMÉ AMIDALA!

ISSUE 142
JULY 2013
U.S. $7.99
Can $9.99

TITAN

FIVE ALIVE!

HOW *STAR WARS: THE CLONE WARS* SEASON FIVE CHANGED THE SAGA!

BEYOND *STAR WARS*

HOW MARVEL COMICS EXPANDED THE SAGA!

PLUS!

VISUAL EFFECTS SECRETS
RETURN OF THE JEDI
THE LATEST BOOKS, COMICS, COLLECTIBLES
& MUCH MORE!

HOWARD CHAYKIN AND ROY THOMAS

MARVEL COMICS

ISSUE 142
JULY 2013

Reaching newsstands before the movie on which it was based hit theaters in May 1977, Marvel's *Star Wars* comic book was the introduction to George Lucas' bold new galaxy for many sci-fi aficionados. It's a bit of a push to suggest that Jaxxon, the green rabbit-like character who appeared in early issues, is iconic, but the combination of Roy Thomas' no-nonsense storytelling and Howard Chaykin's striking art style presents a memorable take on the saga.**—Jonathan Wilkins**

Roy William Thomas, Jr. *was born on November 22, 1940 in Jackson, Missouri. He was Stan Lee's successor as editor-in-chief of Marvel Comics and has served as an editor and writer at DC and Marvel, working with characters such as Spider-Man, Superman, Batman, Doctor Strange, Captain America, the X-Men and the Avengers. He was inducted into the Will Eisner Comic Book Hall of Fame in 2011.*

Howard Victor Chaykin *was born on October 7, 1950 in Newark, New Jersey. After high school, he became an assistant to the respected comic-book artist Gil Kane, whom he would later name as his greatest influence. He published his first professional comics work in 1971 and began working for DC and Marvel the following year. In the 1980s, he created* American Flagg! *for First Comics.*

AUTHORS OF THE EXPANDED UNIVERSE:
ROY THOMAS AND HOWARD CHAYKIN

BY MICHAEL KOGGE

It is a period of *CIVIL WAR* in the galaxy. A brave alliance of *UNDERGROUND FREEDOM FIGHTERS* has challenged the tyranny and oppression of the awesome *GALACTIC EMPIRE*. To CRUSH the rebellion once and for all, *the EMPIRE* is constructing a sinister new *BATTLE STATION*. Powerful enough *to destroy* an entire planet, *its COMPLETION* will spell *CERTAIN DOOM* for the *champions* of freedom...

This was the introductory crawl of a certain film's rough cut that comics writer Roy Thomas and illustrator Howard Chaykin saw in February 1977, a crawl which Thomas would use to open Marvel Comics' adaptation of "The Greatest Space-Fantasy Film of All!"—*Star Wars*.

Those first words of that first issue would lead to an unprecedented marriage of a comic book and a film franchise for almost 10 years. *Star Wars*, under the aegis of Marvel, would run uninterrupted for 107 monthly issues, and 3 annuals, from March 1977 to September 1986. Its commercial success, according to one Marvel editor-in-chief, saved the company from financial ruin. Moreover, the series continues to charm new fans years later with Dark Horse's reprints.

Odd it might seem, then, that Marvel's *Star Wars* almost never launched.

STAND BY TO LOCK "S-FOILS" IN ATTACK POSITIONS!

BLUE TWO STANDING BY, BLUE LEADER.

BLUE THREE STANDING BY.

BLUE FOUR STANDING BY.

BLUE FIVE STANDING BY.

BLUE SIX STANDING BY.

ZZRR! ZAR!

ROY THOMAS HAD SHEPHERDED THE CREATION OF NOW-CLASSIC CHARACTERS SUCH AS WOLVERINE.

Roy Thomas: The Origin Story

By the time he met George Lucas in early 1975, Roy Thomas had worked in comics for nearly a decade. He had begun his professional life as a high school English teacher in Missouri, but his boyhood passion for comics compelled him to move to New York to try to make it in the industry. When a job as an assistant editor at DC Comics wasn't what he had dreamed it'd be, Thomas sent a letter to a writer-editor whose work he adored: Marvel's Stan Lee, offering to buy him a drink. Lee called back with an even better proposition: Would Thomas like to take Marvel's writing test? After adding his own dialogue to word balloons in the *Fantastic Four*, Thomas was hired as a Marvel staff writer.

Thomas went from scripting the romance comic *Modeling with Millie* to superhero titles such as *Doctor Strange* and *X-Men*, on the way up the company ladder. In 1972, when Lee became Marvel's publisher, Thomas succeeded him as editor-in-chief, shepherding the creation of now-classic characters such as Wolverine and Ghost Rider. He resigned in August 1974 to concentrate on freelance work, specifically the titles he had convinced Marvel to license based on Robert E. Howard's Conan novels. At the time, George Lucas was a frequent visitor to Edward Summer's Supersnipe Comic Art Emporium in Manhattan. Summer knew that Thomas, his neighbor, admired Lucas's *American Graffiti* and that Lucas, in turn, was a fan of Thomas's writing, so he invited the men out to dinner (see *The Best of Star Wars Insider Volume 2* for an extended interview with Summer).

I-- --DARTH VADER!

ZZRAKK

THE SITH LORD BRINGS HIS SWORD DOWN, SEEMINGLY CUTTING HIS ELDER FOE IN HALF!

BEN KENOBI'S CLOAK FALLS TO THE FLOOR IN TWO PARTS--

THONGOR
IN THE
CITY OF MAGICIANS

Thongor battles the satanic power of Zaar's science and sorcery—armed only with his Valkarthan broadsword

LIN CARTER

Spaghetti Dinners and Space Operas

Discussion during the meal soon turned to the "space fantasy" film Lucas was developing, which had a working title of *The Star Wars*. The fact that Lucas was taking his movie so seriously, with such respect to the genre, enthused Thomas. As a youth, Thomas had been an avid reader of science fiction, particularly of *Planet Comics*, and Lucas's film seemed to share those roots. The men ended up at Thomas's apartment, chatting the night away about comics and marveling at the original Frazetta painting, *Thor's Flight*, that Thomas owned.

Busy with his freelance work, Thomas thought little more of that evening until months later when Summer brought Charley Lippincott, Lucasfilm's vice-president of marketing and merchandising, to his place. Lippincott had been touring the country promoting *Star Wars* at comic book conventions, wooing thousands of fans. But he had yet to seduce the most important fans of all: the comic industry executives who could fill-in the "yes" balloons. All three major publishers—D.C., Jim Warren Publishing, and Marvel—rebuffed proposals to turn *Star Wars* into a comic book series.

Recognizing that Thomas's talents in the sword-and-sorcery genre would translate well to *Star Wars*, Lippincott offered Thomas the opportunity to adapt the property. He also ventured that securing Thomas, once one of Marvel's higher-ups, might get this unknown space fantasy film a second look from the top brass.

Thomas listened politely as Lippincott showed "production drawings" and pitched the story of "Luke Starkiller," stormtroopers, and a wizard who sounded Japanese given his name, Obi-Wan Kenobi. While intriguing, other movie properties like *Planet of the Apes* had caused Thomas considerable headaches at Marvel, and he understood why the publishers had refused. "Science fiction didn't have much of a track record in comics. In the '50s they'd tried a lot of it, and it didn't do well," Thomas says.

But his reluctance changed when Lippincott pulled out a Ralph McQuarrie painting of the cantina scene. One look at the aliens, robots, and brash smuggler reminded Thomas of the space fantasies of his youth. He jumped to adapt the series.

Thomas was now Lucasfilm's new hope—perhaps their only hope—to make *Star Wars* a Marvel comic book. But if he wanted this job, he'd have to convince Stan Lee.

PUT YOUR BLASTERS AWAY. MEN!

HAN, MY BOY, I'M ONLY DOING THIS BECAUSE YOU'RE THE *BEST*, AND I *NEED* YOU.

BUT, IF YOU DISAPPOINT ME *AGAIN*, I'LL PUT A *PRICE* ON YOUR HEAD SO *LARGE*--

From opposite page, clockwise: Han Solo in action; the rebel pilots prepare their assault on the Death Star; Ralph McQuarrie's cantina painting which proved instrumental in getting Roy Thomas onboard; Frank Frazetta's *Thor's Flight*, featured here on the cover of *Thongor in the City of Magicians* by Lin Carter, helped create a bond between Thomas and George Lucas; Jabba the Hut (sic) threatens Han, but isn't quite himself as nobody quite knew how he would look when Howard Chaykin was illustrating the strip; Darth Vader defeats Obi-Wan Kenobi in a typically dramatic panel.

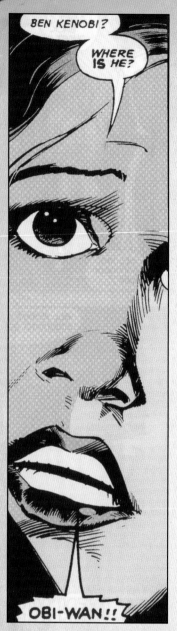

BEN KENOBI?

WHERE IS HE?

OBI-WAN!!

"This is the Comic Book You're Looking For..."

Thomas went to Lee with Conan under his belt, having turned it into one of Marvel's best-selling titles. He might be able to make *Star Wars* successful where Marvel's previous excursions into science-fiction had floundered. Furthermore, Lee wouldn't be taking that big of a gamble financially. The license fees were virtually non-existent, given that Lucasfilm's main objective was to get *Star Wars* into print. What really seemed to hook Lee, however, was that the actor playing the wizard with the Japanese-sounding name was none other than Alec Guinness. While this bit of casting would never sell an issue, Lee loved Guinness's work, and likely thought there could be something to Lucas's film. He assigned Thomas to both write and edit the adaptation. No one in Marvel could overrule Lee's decision. But Ed Shukin, director of circulation, wasn't confident the book would sell, especially with Lucasfilm's insistence that the first two issues be out before the film was released. Wanting to cut the potential losses, Shukin recommended Thomas adapt the book as one or two issues. Thomas refused, believing *Star Wars* deserved more than a 32-page treatment as in the old Gold Key movie adaptations. Either *Star Wars* would be six issues or they could find another writer.

Marvel stuck with Thomas.

--BEN'S OWN LIGHTSABRE COMES SUDDENLY TO LIFE--

--AND A WIDE-EYED LUKE SKYWALKER IS ABRUPTLY REMINDED THAT OLD BEN KENOBI WAS ONCE OBI-WAN KENOBI--

--A JEDI KNIGHT!

GNG

FZZT!

...WE WILL DISCUSS THE LOCATION OF THE *HIDDEN REBEL BASE*.

STRETCH OUT WITH YOUR FEEL- INGS, LUKE-- IN THE DARK!

"I REGARD [MY WORK ON *STAR WARS*] AS GOING TO SCHOOL IN PUBLIC."
—HOWARD CHAYKIN

"Always Two There Are"

Finding an artist to illustrate the comic was much easier. Lucas had been following the career of Howard Chaykin because the young New Yorker was storyboarding a movie Edward Summer intended to make, *Starship Under*. Chaykin seemed the ideal choice: His mentor was the legendary Gil Kane; he had created a character Lucas loved, space pirate "Lord Ironwolf" for DC's *Weird Worlds*; and he was exceptional at drawing futuristic technology. Armed with the screenplay and some production stills, Chaykin dove into the assignment to pencil and ink all six issues. The contract stipulated that the first book be on newsstands by March 1977, so Thomas told Chaykin to break down the screenplay into six dramatic arcs and start drawing immediately. Chaykin would finish penciled pages in batches, to which Thomas would then script narration and dialogue for the letterer to add. The lettered pages would then be shipped back to Chaykin for inking, a cycle that couldn't stop until the series was completed.

Chaykin captured the swashbuckling tone of *Star Wars* at once, having also grown up reading classic science-fiction. But the 24-year-old soon realized he lacked the speed to complete the series on deadline. Since the movie was in postproduction while he was drawing, he also had little material available for reference. "I was flying by the seat of my pants," Chaykin says, looking back at the work. "I regard it as going to school in public."

Steve Leialoha came aboard to help, first as an inker, then embellishing Chaykin's rough layouts for the next four issues. Chaykin acknowledges today that Leialoha's contributions "pulled that stuff together...[he] did far better work on that stuff than I did." Nonetheless, even with assistance, the production slowed. For the final issue, artists Rick Hoberg and Bill Wray brought Chaykin's roughs to completion, doing it all in the span of a week, with little sleep.

Left: Luke and Leia swing into action!
Below and right: The first *Star Wars* sequel, as issue #7 took the story beyond the movie!

Opposite page, from top: Jaxxon, a cult favorite, but not so popular with George Lucas; the Death Star strikes!

Saving Marvel Comics

Star Wars didn't flame out like other science-fiction comic books, perhaps because it was more of an adventure story, a space fantasy. The series became one of Marvel's hottest titles, with *Star Wars* #1 eventually reaching more than a million copies sold.

The late 1970s were a rough patch when Marvel couldn't move their superhero books as they could in the past, so they leaned on *Star Wars*, reprinting the comic in every form, from special-sized tabloids to an "illustrated" paperback for bookstores. No executive balked at the license fee Lucasfilm asked for after those six issues ran their course; Marvel wanted to keep this moneymaker in-house. Jim Shooter, Marvel's editor-in-chief in 1978, has even claimed that it was *Star Wars* that kept Marvel Comics financially afloat during those difficult times.

JIM SHOOTER, MARVEL'S EDITOR-IN-CHIEF, CLAIMED STAR WARS KEPT MARVEL COMICS AFLOAT...

Of Rogues and Rabbits

S*tar Wars'* life as a monthly continuing series necessitated the creation of an ongoing narrative that continued after the events of the film. To make sure these new tales did not conflict with potential movie sequels, Lucasfilm restricted what could be done, particularly with Luke and Leia. Han Solo was granted the most freedom, so Thomas took the smuggler and Chewbacca on an adventure reminiscent of *The Magnificent Seven*.

After the first couple of issues of an arc now known as the "Starhoppers of Aduba-3", Lippincott phoned to say that Lucasfilm did not like the direction of the series. Not only was the plot too similar to *The Magnificent Seven*, Lucas didn't think Jaxxon, a green Bugs Bunny–type character inspired by a *Porky Pig* alien Thomas swore he saw during the film's rough cut, fit into the *Star Wars* pantheon. Thomas felt a space rabbit wasn't all that different from the ape-like Chewbacca, but he also understood that this wasn't his universe. Meanwhile, Chaykin was veering off into other projects, and most of his *Star Wars* pages were being ghost-penciled by Alan Kupperberg. Both Chaykin and Thomas figured this would be a good time to step away, and so by issue #11, the *Star Wars* comic was being written by Archie Goodwin and drawn by Carmine Infantino and Terry Austin.

Old Starhoppers Never Die

A s new generations of fans re-discover Roy Thomas and Howard Chaykin's run in the Marvel comics, those first expanded universe tales continue to fuel intense debate, even 36 years after publication. "What I appreciate most about Roy's story is that it continues the idea of *Star Wars* being a pastiche," says Lucasfilm's Pablo Hidalgo, who wrote an article about the Starhoppers for *Star Wars Gamer* magazine. "Roy combines old cartoons, Westerns, Samurai films, and Japanese monster movies into one tale. Since there was so little to go on, the Marvel team really had to create things from scratch, and you see that in the wild creativity of that storyline."*Star Wars* proved to be one of many highlights in the storied careers of Thomas and Chaykin. Thomas went on to script hundreds more comics, and co-write the screenplays for *Fire and Ice* (1983) and *Conan the Destroyer* (1984), and was inducted in the Eisner Comic Book Hall of Fame. Among many other original series, Chaykin created the award-winning *American Flagg!* in the 1980s, and is now writing and drawing *Buck Rogers* for Hermes Press.

As for future stories of the green bunny? Roy says, "I'd love it. It'd be fun to get another crack at doing *Star Wars* all these years later."

Fans of the Starhoppers, now is the time to comm in your requests! ☮

Special thanks to Roy Thomas, Howard Chaykin, Rick Hoberg, John Morrow, and Pablo Hidalgo. Roy Thomas's personal recollection of his work on *Star Wars* appears in *Alter Ego* #68 (TwoMorrows Publishing).

ROY THOMAS SELECT BIBLIOGRAPHY

Star Wars Omnibus: A Long Time Volume 1 (Dark Horse)
The Savage Sword of Conan (Dark Horse reprints)
Marvel Visionaries: Roy Thomas (Marvel compilation)
Roy Thomas Presents line of vintage comics (PS Publishing)
Current editor of *Alter Ego* comics magazine (TwoMorrows Publishing)

HOWARD CHAYKIN SELECT BIBLIOGRAPHY

Star Wars Omnibus: A Long Time Volume 1 (Dark Horse)
The Art of Howard Chaykin (ed. Robert Greenberger, Dynamite Entertainment)
American Flagg! (Image Comics)
Time²: The Epiphany (First Comics)

THE OFFICIAL MAGAZINE OF THE *STAR WARS* SAGA

ALL-NEW FICTION! An Exclusive Adventure, Inside!

STAR WARS

®

HERE'S HERA!

Star Wars Rebels' Vanessa Marshall Talks Season Two

WINGMEN!

Star Wars' Flying Aces Take Flight!

50 COOL THINGS YOU MAY HAVE MISSED IN STAR WARS: THE FORCE AWAKENS!

ISSUE #165
US $7.99
CAN $9.99
MAY/JUNE 2016

TITAN

ROGER CHRISTIAN
LIGHTSABER

ISSUE 165
MAY/JUN 2016

Bloodline released

Ultimate Factivity Collection: LEGO Star Wars released

Star Wars Graphics released

Star Wars: The Phantom Menace hardcover released

Star Wars: Obi-Wan & Anakin #5 released

Finn's Mission released

The Adventures of BB-8 released

Finn and Poe Team Up! released

When he came to create *Star Wars*, George Lucas assembled a team of geniuses. Their talent created a film that has withstood the test of time and become loved and cherished by generation after generation. One of those geniuses was set dresser Roger Christian, who was instrumental in putting together the distinctive "used universe" look of *A New Hope*, setting the standard for the world of *Star Wars* to this day.

This feature includes an exclusive photograph of Roger's original mock-up lightsaber prop. I'm proud to say that Roger very kindly let me hold this prop —a priceless *Star Wars* artifact! It's much heavier than it looks. I could really feel the weight of movie history when I held it in my hand.—**Jonathan Wilkins**

Roger Christian *was born on February 25, 1944 in the United Kingdom. He has worked as a set decorator, production designer, and director on numerous film and TV projects including* Alien *(1979),* Monty Python's Life of Brian *(1979), and* The Young Indiana Jones Chronicles *(1992-1993). He received an Academy Award for his work on the original* Star Wars *and was Oscar-nominated for his work on* Alien. *Christian's feature films include* The Sender *(1982),* Nostradamus *(1994) , and* Battlefield Earth *(1999).*

ROGER CHRISTIAN REVEALS THE MOMENT HE FOUND LUKE'S LIGHTSABER WHILE WORKING ON *STAR WARS* IN THIS EXCLUSIVE ADAPTED EXCERPT FROM HIS NEW BOOK, *CINEMA ALCHEMIST*.

*A*s set decorator on Star Wars: A New Hope, *my intention was to create a world that was used and real. During* my first conversation with George Lucas in Mexico, he described the movie as a space western. I immediately understood what he wanted. Our common ground were the spaghetti westerns of Sergio Leone, made for tiny budgets in the southern deserts of Spain. Production designer John Barry took George to Tunisia and showed him the ancient desert civilization that looked exactly like George's descriptions of Tatooine.

In the following extract, adapted from my book Cinema Alchemist, *I describe how I came upon the Graflex flash handles, ending my search for Luke's lightsaber.*

Brunnings, the photographic shop on Great Marlborough Street, sold a huge array of new and second-hand equipment. I asked David French, the manager of the shop, if they had any old or damaged equipment I could buy for a movie I was working on. He pointed me to boxes of equipment that had obviously lain untouched for years. I started rummaging through them and found old lenses and rangefinders, pulling out anything I thought might be useful. I then discovered one old box under the others, covered in dust, that obviously had not been opened for years.

It was an auspicious moment. In a movie the music would be heralding a major climactic incident was about to erupt, and it would be in slow motion.

OF INSPIRATION

There, before my eyes, were several silver, tube-like objects with red buttons set into the handles, packed in tissue paper.

I pulled one out, amazed. They actually looked like Ralph McQuarrie's paintings of the lightsaber. Somehow I was at the moment of finding the Holy Grail. Even the red firing button seemed perfectly designed for a lightsaber handle. I held one in my hand; it was the right weight and size. I had found the treasure that was eluding me, and I knew exactly what to do with it as I headed straight back to Elstree Studios.

I went to my room and closed the door. I got out my supply of black rubber t-strip, the same kind I had used when creating the stormtrooper's blaster, and altered it to look like a weapon handle. I cut the t-section rubber carefully to the desired length and shaped the ends to look finished. I stuck each of the seven strips, evenly spaced, around the handle. I found an old strip of LED lights from a scrap Texas Instruments calculator; I liked the look of the strip of plastic bubbles used to magnify the numbers. They fitted exactly into the small mounting clip so that it looked like another function of the lightsaber. I superglued the plastic strip on to the Graflex, and there, before my eyes, was Luke's lightsaber. I placed a strip of chrome tape around the shaft to hide the Graflex name, and then added a small D-ring so it could hang from a belt. The elegant weapon was finally ready to make its on-screen debut in Obi-Wan Kenobi's hut! ☢

TITAN
ISSUE #153
US $7.99
CAN $9.99
NOV/DEC 2014

Display Until
December 9th
2014

DESIGNING WORLDS: THE ART OF *STAR WARS REBELS*

STAR WARS
INSIDER

STAR WEARS
Amazing
Never-Before-Seen
**STAR WARS
COSTUMES**
Revealed!

DARK TIMES
Creating Star Wars Rebels'
EMPIRE OF EVIL!

SITH
BUSTERS!
**The Jedi
Face Their
Deadliest
Foes, Inside!**

COSTUMES
THE ORIGINAL TRILOGY

ISSUE 153
NOV/DEC 2014

A big part of the visual appeal in the *Star Wars* saga comes from the costumes. In 2014, the publication of the book *Star Wars Costumes: The Original Trilogy* afforded fans a closer look at the iconic outfits and how they were created. For its part, *Insider* contributed to the celebration of all things costume with an eight-part overview, starting in issue #153, showing the incredible talent and artistry that went in to creating even the most minor background character's wardrobe. That entire series is collected here.—**Jonathan Wilkins**

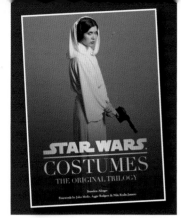

STAR WARS STYLE

COSTUMES
FOR A GALAXY FAR, FAR AWAY

INSIDER TAKES A LOOK AT SOME OF THE TREASURES INSIDE THE *STAR WARS* WARDROBE ARCHIVES IN AN EXCLUSIVE REPORT BY AUTHOR BRANDON ALINGER.

I n writing *Star Wars Costumes: The Original Trilogy* (Chronicle Books, October 28, 2014), I had a rare opportunity to conduct an in-depth examination of a specific facet of a film series produced decades ago. What other movies would ever receive such treatment? The outfits showcased in the book belong to characters who have become ingrained into popular culture—and why shouldn't they be? As costume designer Deborah Nadoolman-Landis (who is responsible for outfitting another famed Lucasfilm adventurer, Indiana Jones) said, "Costumes are so much more than clothes, embodying the psychological, social and emotional condition of the character at a particular moment in the script. The costume designer gives the clothes to the actor, the actor gives the character to the director, and the director tells the story. Cinematic icons are born when the audience falls deeply in love with the people in the story. And that's what movies, and costume design, are all about."

The original trilogy's costumes warranted a book of their own, as their creation tale is enormously complex. Just as *Star Wars* was no ordinary film series, the saga's costumes are not your typical ensembles. Over the course of the trilogy, three costumes designers—John Mollo, Aggie Rodgers, and Nilo Rodis-Jamero—and dozens of technicians, wardrobe personnel, and outside vendors worked diligently to bring authentic characters to life through their costumes. "The costumes from *Star Wars* are really not so much costumes as bits of plumbing and general automobile engineering," said *A New Hope* costume designer John Mollo while accepting the Academy Award for the film.

The results of the designers' work speak for themselves not only in the success of the films, but in the success of their merchandising. The legion of *Star Wars* action figures could be described as little more than miniature versions of the costumes.

Here is a preview of some of the stories told in *Star Wars Costumes: The Original Trilogy*, published by Chronicle Books and released October 28, 2014.

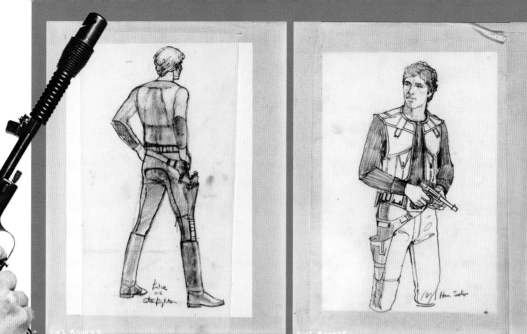

Like much of the film's design, the earliest renditions of *A New Hope*'s costumes were created by Ralph McQuarrie. McQuarrie looked at westerns as one of his influences, as evidenced by the gunslinger belts. These sketches bear handwritten titles by George Lucas.

For the film's final ceremony, Lucas wanted Luke to be dressed more like Han Solo. As such, he was a given a pair of trousers with the distinctive segmented tuxedo stripe. The brown-and-yellow trousers, identical to Solo's in *Empire* and *Jedi*, were identified by the archivists at Skywalker Ranch while researching for the costume book. The giveaway is the 28" waist size, 4" smaller than Ford's trousers.

Working on a limited budget, Mollo assembled many costumes from stock garment pieces found at Bermans and Nathans, the leading costume house in London at the time. With more than a million costume pieces in stock, Bermans had the variety that Mollo needed to assemble garb for a galaxy far, far away. Some of the pieces in their stock had been in use as theatrical rental pieces since the late 18th century. One of Bermans and Nathans' original window signs today hangs on the wall at Angels the Costumiers, who acquired Bermans and Nathans in 1992.

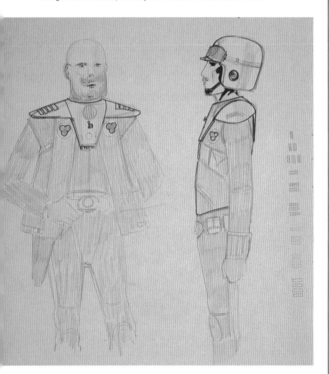

John Mollo was an ideal choice to design costumes for *A New Hope* as he had an extensive background in military uniforms. "George said to me, 'You've got a very difficult job here. I don't want anyone to notice the costumes,'" Mollo recalled. In this early Mollo sketch for rebel aides and field commanders, the designer's usage of military-like insignia is apparent. The insignia, including the well-known rebel and Imperial emblems, became a staple of many *Star Wars* uniforms.

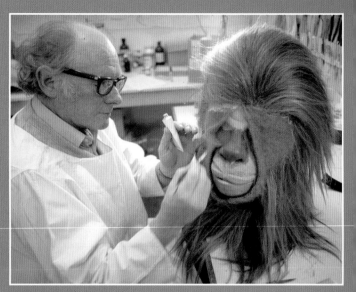

A New Hope could not have been produced without a major collaborative effort from the various departments. For Chewbacca, a body suit was knitted under the supervision of the costume department from Angora wool, and knotted with hand-tied yak hair. The Wookiee mask was created by veteran industry make-up artist Stuart Freeborn, who had built a similar mask for the apes in *2001: A Space Odyssey*. The moustache-like cuts seen here in the Wookiee's upper lip helped the snarl mechanism of the mask function as intended.

Chewbacca's mask featured an integral hood, knitted and knotted in the same fashion as the body suit. Here is Stuart Freeborn's original pattern for the hood.

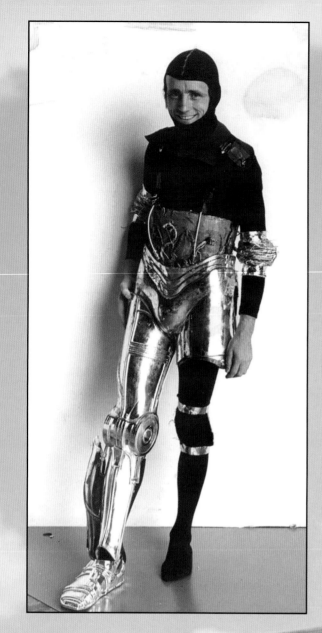

C-3PO's golden shell may have been the most complex costume created for any *Star Wars* film. "It was first offered to the costume department, but they said 'That's far too industrial.' So it was handed off to the prop department," says prop man Brian Lofthouse, who dressed Anthony Daniels in the costume. The suit went on in many components and required a lot of engineering work to function correctly. These images, featuring prop man Jim Marlow in the suit, show how it went together. Note the wires crudely taped on where the openings in the joints could potentially show — these were upgraded to stitched fabric versions for *Jedi*.

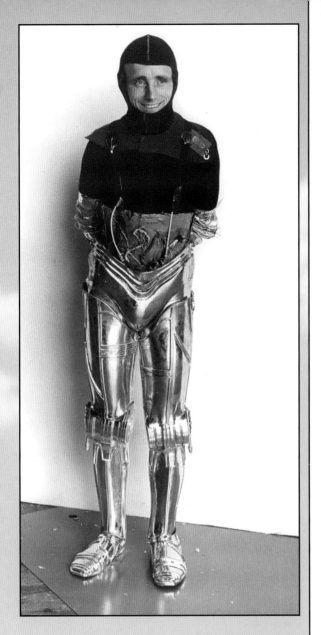

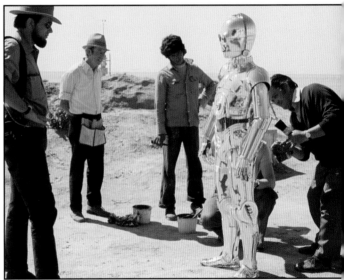

Wardrobe assistant Colin Wilson dressed many actors on the set of *A New Hope*. He is seen here preparing a rebel pilot for battle. "Most of the costumes were quite easy to look after," says Wilson. "It was only the stormtroopers that proved a bit of a headache."

Final assembly of the C-3PO costume was completed on location the night before cameras rolled. Here a painter prepares to dress the costume with wax and grime to prevent it from reflecting an on-set "chippie" (carpenter) or "spark" (electrician) into the camera.

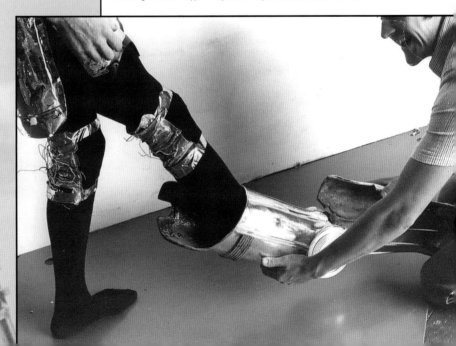

Mollo experimented with a wide variety of styles for the Imperial Officers' cap. The "Imperial disc" that adorns the cap in the final film is actually a pulley from an LP turntable manufactured in Borehamwood, not far from Elstree Studios where the original trilogy was shot.

Stormtrooper costumes were manufactured by "vacuum-forming" sheet plastic. The vacuum-forming process involves heating a piece of plastic, and then using suction to form it over a pattern. The stormtrooper costumes were notoriously difficult to wear, let alone sit down in.

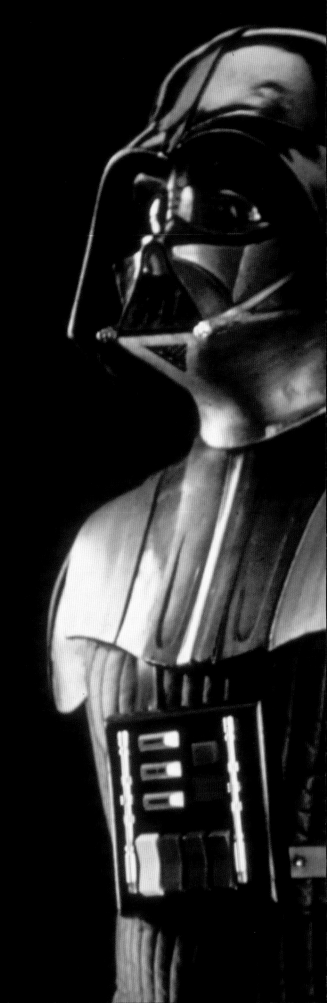

The Darth Vader costume used in *A New Hope* was sent to Don Post Studios for a brief time after production, to serve as reference for the Vader Halloween masks they were producing. This image was taken outside of Don Post Studios, and offers a rare close-up of the helmet.

"George wanted the Imperials to look very efficient, and totalitarian, and Fascist," said Mollo. The designer's original plan for the Imperial Officers was to repurpose tunics from the film *The Blue Max*, as pictured here. "We played with the idea of taking all the buttons off, but Bermans decided that they didn't want their uniforms messed about in that way," said Mollo.

STAR WARS STYLE

T he costumes of *The Empire Strikes Back* were the most difficult to research for *Star Wars Costumes: The Original Trilogy* (available now from Chronicle Books). No archival interviews on the subject were available, and tracking down members of the film's costume department was difficult. Fortunately, costume designer John Mollo was happy to chat and invited me to spend a day at his home near Oxford, in England, where we waded through photographs and discussed the designer's final *Star Wars* film. *Empire* was a more challenging film for Mollo than *A New Hope*. He began, as he had on the first film, with a small number of concept sketches that were sent over from the US. Key concept artists Ralph McQuarrie and Joe Johnston had started working on designs for the sequel just months after the first film's release. The pair explored the visual dynamic of the new worlds—Hoth and Cloud City—and completed some costume concepts as part of that study. Notably, the designs for the snowtroopers and Boba Fett were established during this period. But the vast majority of the costumes were to be worked out by Mollo. Beyond updating the look of the returning characters, the English designer had to create new garb for a variety of new characters who would appear on Hoth and Cloud City. While the costumes of the first film had been very nondescript, he felt the sequel needed something

more. "I had a tendency to make the designs slightly more interesting on this film," says Mollo. "I was hoping to get in a slight enrichment of things." Mollo began sketching away with this in mind, and produced a huge number of illustrations. He found it more difficult to get decisions from director Irvin Kershner and producer Gary Kurtz than he had working directly with George Lucas on the original film. As such, many wildly different directions were considered for the costumes of *Empire*. These were explored through both physical prototypes (which Kershner and Kurtz liked to see) and Mollo's numerous sketches. The unused concepts are fascinating as they are frequently far more intricate and elaborate than the final costumes.

So... read on for a taste of some of *Empire*'s war stories from the frozen plains of Hoth!

▼The designer envisioned expanding the ranks of the rebel forces. The outfits depicted in these sketches were distilled down to just a few basic outfits for officers and technicians.

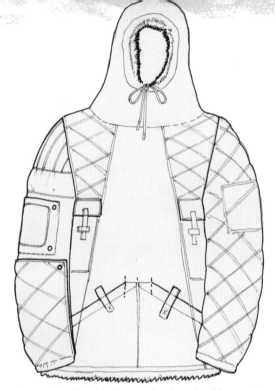

▲The snow jacket of the rebel soldiers went through a number of design revisions as well. Here is a line-art version of one design considered. On *Empire*, Mollo did many line-art drawings that could be copied for experimenting with different color schemes. The rebel outfits wound up being some of his favorites in the film.

BASEBALL CAP
HOOD
DUFFLE COAT
FAWN KHAKI OVERALLS
BOOTS
REBEL GENERAL

CLOTH HELMET
KHAKI QUILTED JACKET
KHAKI FAWN OVERALLS
BOOTS
1 CONTROLLERS ETC

CLOTH HELMET
SCARF
LEATHER FLYING JACKET
FLYING HELMET
ORANGE OVERALLS
FLYING BOOTS
5 STARFIGHTER PILOT

LEATHER TANK HELMET
BALACLAVA
KHAKI QUILTED JACKET
GLOVES
BELT + PISTOL HOLSTER
KHAKI OVERALLS
BOOTS
6 LANDSPEEDER CREW

REBEL STEEL HELMET
CLOTH HELMET
BALACLAVA
HOODED ANORAK
BELT + EQUIPMENT
GLOVES
KHAKI OVERALLS
BOOTS
TROOPER OFFICER

PACK
ICE AXE
GROUND SHEET
4 SNOWTROOPER

BASEBALL CAP
CLOTH HELMET
HOODED ANORAK
GLOVES
FAWN OVERALLS
BOOTS
GROUND CREWMAN

STEEL HELMET
CLOTH HELMET
KHAKI QUILTED JACKET
CREAM COMBAT WAISTCOAT
GLOVES
KHAKI OVERALLS
8 STAR CRUISER CREW

▼ Both Joe Johnston's (above right) and Ralph McQuarrie's (above left) art showed the rebel soldiers wearing combat helmets on Hoth, similar to the ones they donned in *A New Hope*. Mollo (below) continued refining the design and considered making the helmets in vacuum-formed plastic.

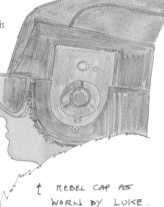

▶Ultimately, the rebel soldiers were given caps rather than helmets. It is not clear whether this was a practical decision (for budget reasons, etc.) or a stylistic one. A cap with a large fin, seen in this Mollo illustration, was considered as a means of distinguishing Luke, but was not used in the end.

↑ REBEL CAP AS WORN BY LUKE.

↑ REBEL CAP

▶Many crew members doubled as extras for sequences shot on location in Norway. Here, associate producer Jim Bloom doubles as a Hoth rebel commando. The outfits were unlined and designed to be worn under hot studio lights, rather than in real frozen terrain.

▲ A number of new R2-D2 units were fabricated for *Empire*, including a few new models for use as a "costume" by Kenny Baker. The interior of one of the droid's domes, seen at left, was decorated to keep Baker entertained during downtime on the set. (Standing at the center is visual effects supervisor Brian Johnson.)

STAR WARS
COSTUMES
THE ORIGINAL TRILOGY

STAR WARS STYLE

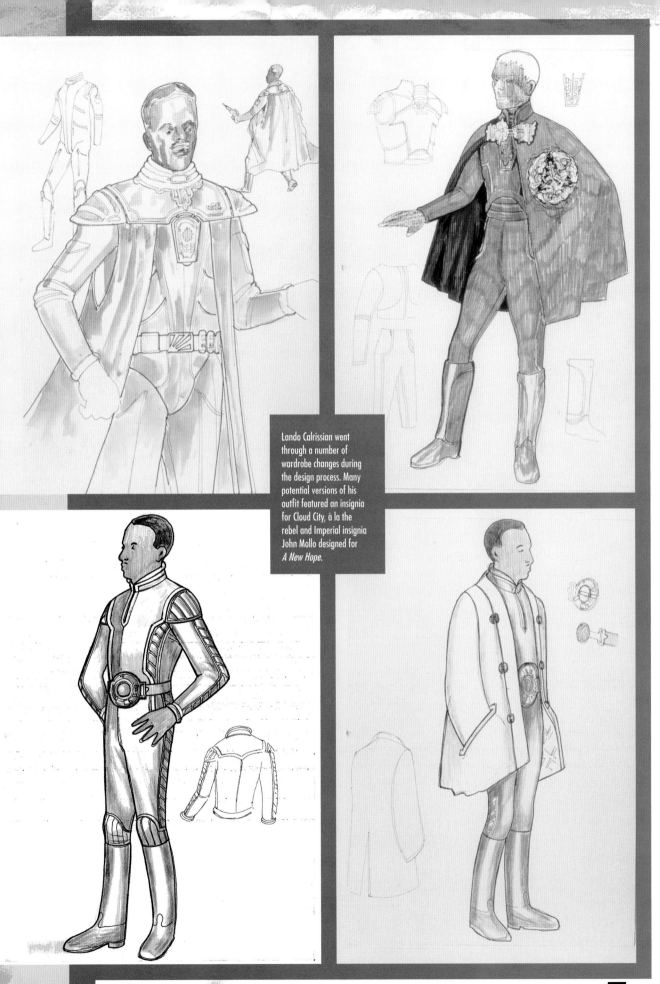

Lando Calrissian went through a number of wardrobe changes during the design process. Many potential versions of his outfit featured an insignia for Cloud City, à la the rebel and Imperial insignia John Mollo designed for *A New Hope.*

2 NAVAL OFFICER   1 ADMIRAL

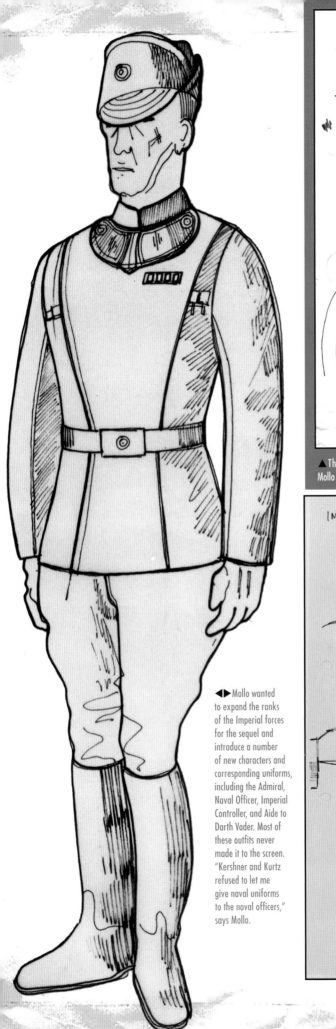

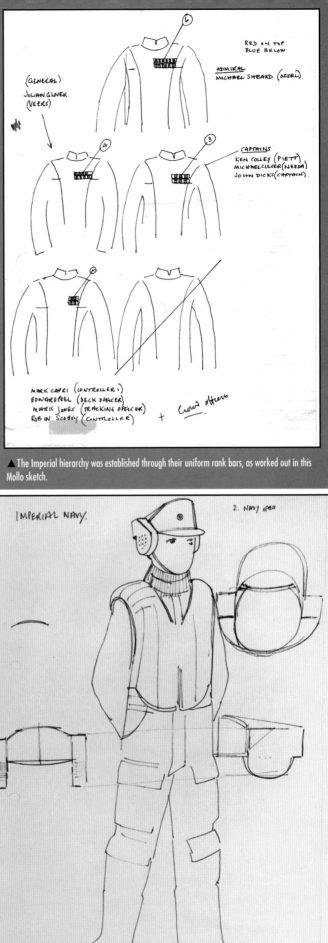

RED ON TOP
BLUE BELOW

ADMIRAL
MICHAEL SHEARD (OZZEL)

(GENERAL)
JULIAN GLOVER
(VEERS)

CAPTAINS
KEN COLLEY (PIETT)
MICHAEL CULVER (NEEDA)
JOHN DICKS (CAPTAIN).

MARK CAPRI (CONTROLLER)
EDWARD PEEL (DECK OFFICER)
MARIK JONES (TRACKING OFFICER)
ROBIN SCOBEY (CONTROLLER)   + CROWD OFFICERS

▲ The Imperial hierarchy was established through their uniform rank bars, as worked out in this Mollo sketch.

IMPERIAL NAVY.   2. NAVY OFFICER

◀▶ Mollo wanted to expand the ranks of the Imperial forces for the sequel and introduce a number of new characters and corresponding uniforms, including the Admiral, Naval Officer, Imperial Controller, and Aide to Darth Vader. Most of these outfits never made it to the screen. "Kershner and Kurtz refused to let me give naval uniforms to the naval officers," says Mollo.

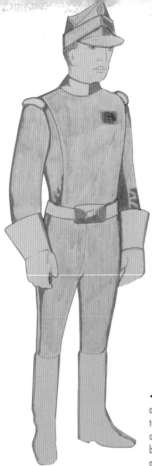

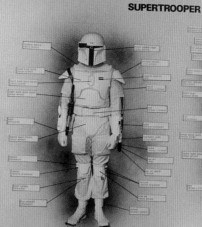

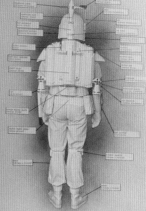

► Boba Fett was a character worked out almost entirely by Joe Johnston and Ralph McQuarrie, though the costumes were still physically built in the UK. The bounty hunter's helmet emerged from sketches by Ralph McQuarrie for a snowtrooper commander, such as this one.

◄ The Cloud City guard was another outfit the team had trouble reaching a consensus on. The costume that went before the cameras was arguably the simplest design.

▼ The bounty hunter's distinctive helmet (center) was painted for *Empire* by Joe Johnston. Additional copies of the helmet, as seen in this shot, were later made for *Jedi*.

The locking mechanism for Vader's helmet dome was revised for the sequel, as seen in this rare shot of the partially dressed Sith Lord.

Sword master Bob Anderson, who handled Darth Vader's dueling duties, wore a specially designed costume. Lifts in the soles of his boots gave him a few extra inches, and a special helmet was designed with a smoked acrylic neckpiece that allowed Anderson to look down and see his feet.

◀ Luke Skywalker's khaki wool jumpsuit was produced in quantity, as the outfit suffers considerable wear and tear in the film. Each stage of distressing, or "breaking down" as it is known in the business, was done by hand in the costume department.

STAR WARS STYLE

Return of the Jedi was to be larger in scope than its predecessors *A New Hope* and *The Empire Strikes Back*, and was designed to move closer to the *Star Wars* universe that George Lucas had always envisioned. The increased scale of the film is evident throughout: Jabba's Palace featured more monsters and guards than the Cantina, the Emperor's arrival featured more troops than any previous *Star Wars* scene, and the space and ground battles included more elements than ever before. It is therefore not surprising that *Jedi*'s costumes occupy nearly half of our book, *Star Wars Costumes: The Original Trilogy*.

The original trilogy's final episode re-used very few costumes from the prior installments. Aggie Rodgers and Nilo Rodis-Jamero were brought on as costume designers, and a *Star Wars* costume shop was established in the same building complex used by Industrial Light & Magic. The majority of the film's costumes were made in-house rather than by outside vendors as they had been in the past (under John Mollo's direction). Legacy costumes that returned essentially the same, such as Darth Vader and the stormtroopers, were manufactured in London under the supervision of the Elstree-based costume team led by Ron Beck, a returning veteran of the first film. As a result of *Jedi*'s costumes being manufactured by the film company directly, more research information was available for the book. In addition to retaining the costumes themselves, the Skywalker Ranch Archives retained original costume design "bibles," meeting notes, fabric samples, reference Polaroids, and muslin mock-ups. The manuscript materials provided key data on facts, figures, and dates, which formed the bedrock of the *Jedi* section of *Star Wars Costumes*. The remaining information came via Aggie Rodgers, Nilo Rodis-Jamero, the many members of the San Rafael-based costume department, and their counterparts on the London side of the film. More available resources meant more information—more than the book could hold. Read on for some fun anecdotes and rare images, many published here for the first time...

► In the initial stages of preproduction, the UK art department began modeling an "enlisted stormtrooper" based on one of Nilo Rodis-Jamero's earliest concepts. The design later evolved into the biker scout, and final costumes were manufactured in the US.

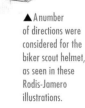

▲ A number of directions were considered for the biker scout helmet, as seen in these Rodis-Jamero illustrations.

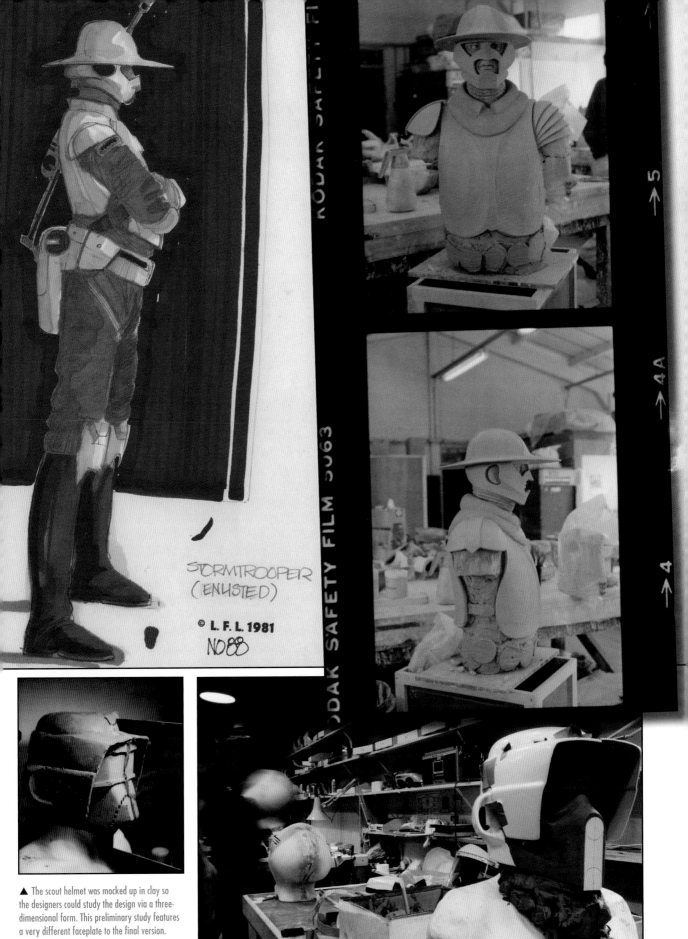

STORMTROOPER
(ENLISTED)

© L. F. L. 1981
NO88

▲ The scout helmet was mocked up in clay so the designers could study the design via a three-dimensional form. This preliminary study features a very different faceplate to the final version.

▶ In the plastic workshop, the final form of the faceplate emerged.

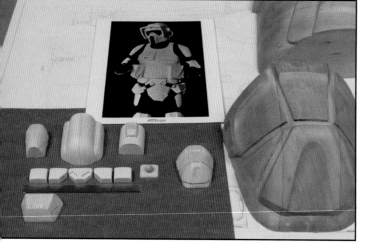

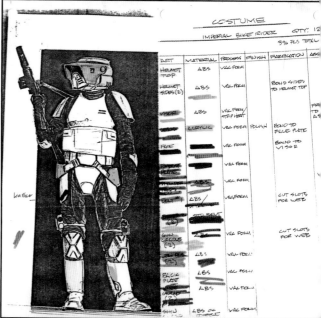

COSTUME

IMPERIAL BIKE RIDER   QTY: 12

396 PCS TOTAL

PART	MATERIAL	PROCESS	FINISH	FABRICATION	ABS
HELMET TOP	ABS	VAC FORM			
HELMET SIDES (2)	ABS	VAC FORM		BOND SIDES TO HELMET TOP	
VISOR	ABS	VAC FORM / STRIP HEAT			
	ACRYLIC	VAC FORM	POLISH	BOND TO FACE PLATE	
FACE		VAC FORM		BOND TO VISOR	
PLATE		VAC FORM			
	ABS			CUT SLOTS FOR WEB	
BELT	ABS /				
	CO-EXT				
		VAC FORM		CUT SLOTS FOR WEB	
GUN CLOVE (2)		VAC FORM			
	ABS	VAC FORM			
BACK PLATE	ABS	VAC FORM			
	ABS	VAC FORM			
GUN	ABS OR OTHER	VAC FORM			

leather

▲ Many of the biker costume components were vacuum-formed from sheets of plastic over wooden forms handcrafted by master pattern maker Ira Keeler. Keeler duplicated his patterns in miniature to produce small-scale costumes for the rod puppets used in the bike chase sequence.

▶ A costume breakdown chart was used by the "plastic boys" to track the components they were responsible for.

Hip armor was prototyped for the biker scout costume, as seen in this fitting photograph, but was dropped from the final design.

▲ The scout costumes were first needed for shooting in the UK, where they appeared on the Death Star docking bay during the Emperor's arrival. The costumes were then shipped back to the US for location work. Dummies were sometimes dressed in biker armor for use on crashing speeder bike props.

▶Costume designers Aggie Rodgers and Nilo Rodis-Jamero experimented with adding some color to Han Solo's wardrobe. A blue shirt was designed as part of the "war room outfit," and the green shirt would have featured on Endor. Both designs were rejected by Harrison Ford. "Ford came in and said he didn't want to wear that. He wanted to look pretty much like he looked in the other two movies," says cutter Claudia Everett.

© L.F.L. 1981

© L.F.L. 1981

"I remember every Friday afternoon, we used to run off to the ranch and we would play baseball. I remember jokingly putting a baseball glove on engineer Wade Childress's head, and that was the birth of Lando Calrissian's disguise," recalls Nilo Rodis-Jamero. Childress posed with the glove, and Rodis-Jamero promptly outlined the rest of the helmet directly onto the Polaroid. Plastic designer Richard Davis holds the final helmet for comparison.

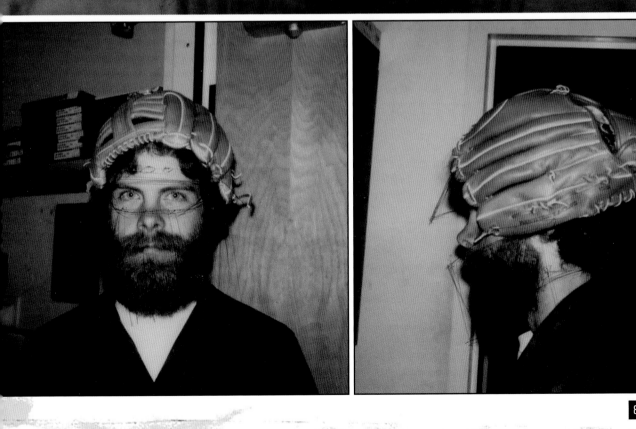

STAR WARS STYLE

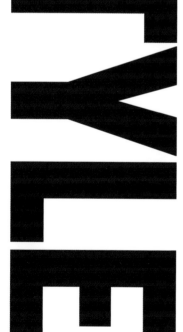

STAR WARS
RETURN OF THE
JEDI

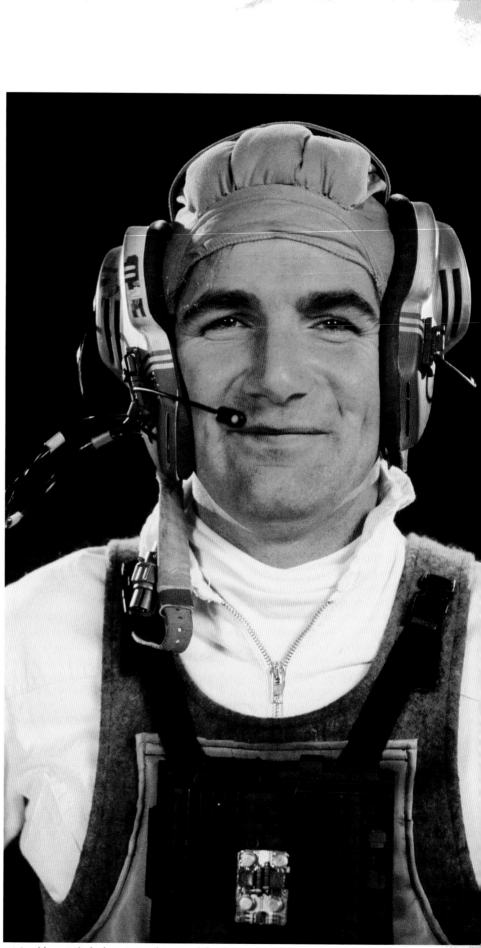

▲ A model poses in the developing A-wing pilot costume, before the jumpsuit was dyed green.

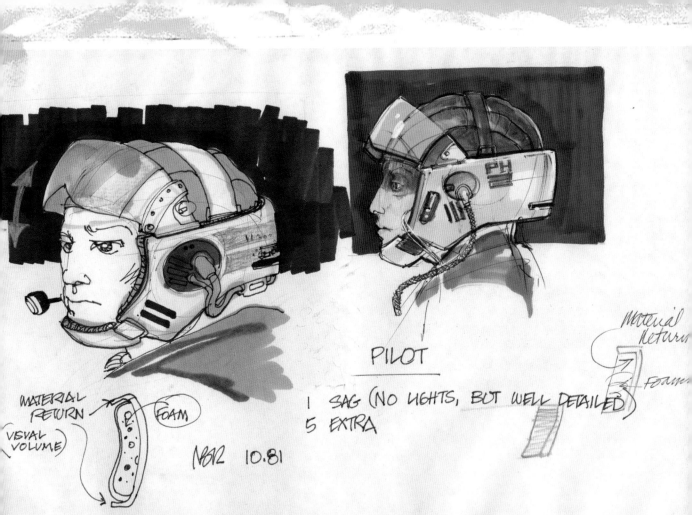

MATERIAL
RETURN
(VISUAL
VOLUME)

FOAM

NBR 10.81

PILOT

1 SAG (NO LIGHTS, BUT WELL DETAILED)
5 EXTRA

Material
Return

Foam

▲ A Nilo Rodis-Jamero illustration for grey (Y-wing) and green (A-wing) pilot helmets questioned whether the helmet visors could be practical.

L.F.L 1981 REBEL
PILOTS

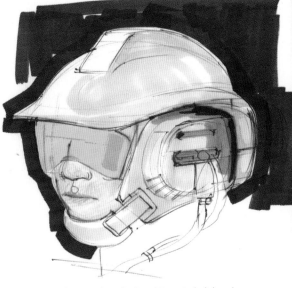

▲ An alternative design for the red (B-wing) pilot helmet shows a hard top shell rather than the soft flight helmet.

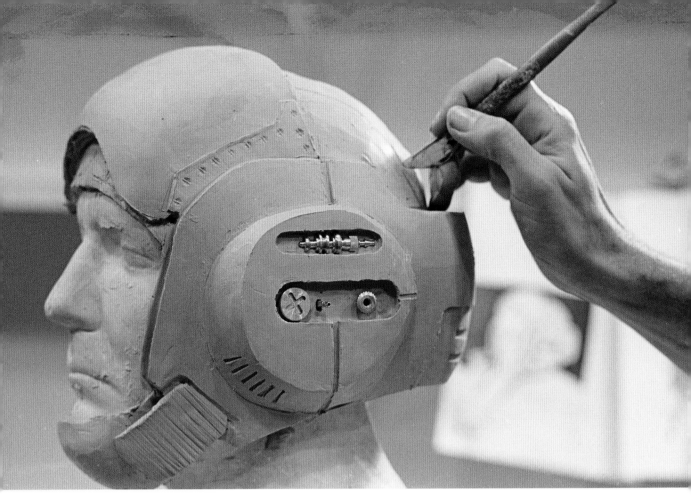

▲ The B-wing pilot helmet design was refined in clay before final patterns were shaped from basswood.
◄ A special B-wing pilot helmet was made specifically for a Sullust alien. In this test photo it is seen with a breathing mask that was not used in the film — the jumpsuit was also not yet dyed red.

FIGHTER PILOTS
HELMET ONLY

NSR 10.81

2

3

© L.F.L. 1981

FIGHTER PILOT

▲ This Rodis-Jamero sketch for the grey (Y-wing) pilot's helmet shows subtle design variances that were considered.

Costume shop manager Jenny Green and accessory technician Mick Becker help dress an Endor rebel commando for a photo shoot.

All of the Endor camouflage was hand-sprayed by textile artist Edwina Pellikka, who experimented with a range of potential colors while honing in on the final design.

▲ In addition to manufacturing hard goods for *Jedi*'s costumes, the plastic boys were responsible for creating various props for the film, including weapons.

BLUE

▶ Ira Keeler poses with a blaster (built around a Kenner toy stormtrooper blaster) intended for use by a monster or skiff guard. This prop never appeared in the final film.

▲ Richard Davis poses with one such probe that was inspired by a Rodis-Jamero illustration for a rebel weapon.

STAR WARS
COSTUMES
THE ORIGINAL TRILOGY

Brandon Alinger
Foreword by John Mollo, Aggie Rodgers & Nilo Rodis-Jamero

STAR WARS STYLE

STAR WARS
RETURN OF THE JEDI

▲ During a costume fitting, costume supervisor Mary Still inspects Carrie Fisher's Endor headgear.

▶ Fisher tries out a muslin prototype of her war room outfit.

►Jabba's dancing girl, Wiebba-Wiebba (later renamed Yarna d'al' Gargan), wore a foam latex prosthetic on her stomach to simulate additional breasts. "Somewhere along the way, in one of those conversations that was beer-induced, we said, 'Oh, and she has six breasts!' And somehow it was appropriate for Jabba's palace," says costume designer Nilo Rodis-Jamero.

▲ Custom headgear was made by costume accessory specialist Barbara Affonso for Jabba's dancers Wiebba-Wiebba (top) and Oola, the Twi'lek dancing girl (bottom).

Gargan

▲ A rare behind-the-scenes shot of stormtrooper stunt performer (second from left) Sandy Gross, pictured here taking a break on location with (from left) Mike Cassidy, Julius Le Flore, and dresser Barbara Affonso, shows that the Imperial forces are not limited to just men.

▶ A fresh set of approximately 50 stormtrooper units was manufactured for *Return of the Jedi*. The costumes were photographed as pristine white outfits in the Death Star sequences, which were shot first, and later dirtied down for use in filming Endor sequences on location.

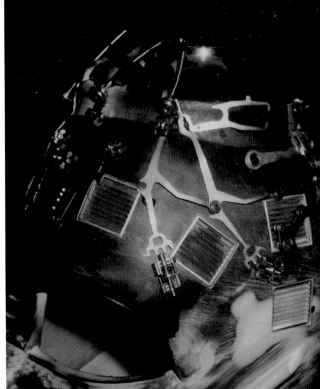

▲ Darth Vader's "reveal" helmet was built by pattern maker Brian Archer at Elstree Studios. These in-progress shots show an alternative greeblie (the pieces added to the basic helmet) configuration to the final piece.

▲ A rare look at the full costume of Ree-Yees — or "Three Eyes" as he was known during production.

▶ One of three Prune Face characters who appeared in the rebel briefing room, this character featured oversized space goggles.

PRUNE FACE

YAK FACE

▲ Yak Face's simple attire is seen in this behind-the-scenes continuity Polaroid.

controllers BUNKER

▲ An Imperial controller, wearing the "cheese grater" helmet originally made for *A New Hope*, and a pair of non-regulation sunglasses.

HUMAN SKIFF GUARD Sc 15

▲ A rarely seen human skiff guard, wearing a helmet made by the "plastic boys" from a modified motorcycle helmet.

Sc 44. LUKE GOES TO X-WING

▲ Mark Hamill adjusts his Tatooine sandstorm goggles in this continuity Polaroid taken during production. The scene — the first to be shot for the movie — was ultimately deleted from the final theatrical version.

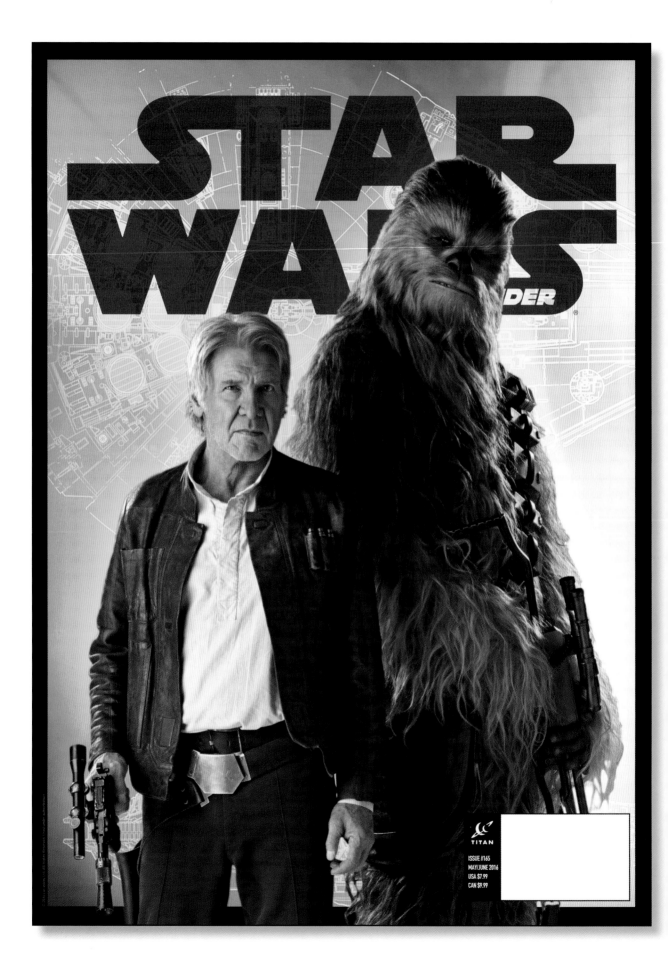

ISSUE #165
MAY/JUNE 2016
USA $7.99
CAN $9.99

OLIVER STEEPLES
DROIDS

ISSUE 165
MAY/JUNE 2016

Sometimes dreams do come true. Oliver Steeples is living proof of this. His story is very simple: an enthusiastic member of the R2 Builders' Club (an amateur organization of fans who scratch-build working R2 units), Oliver took his creations to *Star Wars* Celebration, where they were seen by Lucasfilm boss Kathleen Kennedy. Soon, he and other members of the club were recruited to create droids for the then upcoming film, *Star Wars: The Force Awakens*! As Oliver is such a droid aficionado, we asked him to select the scenes from across the saga where these iconic mechanoids really come into their own.—**Jonathan Wilkins**

Oliver Steeples *is a member of the R2 Builders Club, a fan organization dedicated to building working versions of the droids from the* Star Wars *franchise. Steeples and his friends and fellow builders now create working astromech droids at Pinewood Studios for use in the* Star Wars *movies.*

RED FIVE

OLIVER STEEPLES' FIVE FAVORITE DROID MOMENTS IN THE STAR WARS SAGA

DROID BUILDER OLIVER STEEPLES IS PART OF THE TEAM PERSONALLY APPROACHED BY KATHLEEN KENNEDY TO CREATE DROIDS FOR *STAR WARS: THE FORCE AWAKENS*. SO, WHO BETTER TO NOMINATE FIVE GREAT MOMENTS FEATURING *STAR WARS'* MECHANICAL MARVELS?

① R2-D2 AND C-3PO ON TATOOINE (*A NEW HOPE*, 1977)

The scene with R2-D2 and C-3PO "discussing" which direction to go after landing on Tatooine—the easier, open desert route or the rocky canyon—perfectly sums up their relationship, while exemplifying R2's resolute character. R2 beeps and whistles about his mission and heads off on his own with dogged determination. Even after being captured by Jawas and sold to Owen Lars, the little droid is still dedicated to finding Obi-Wan Kenobi and delivering Princess Leia's message. As Luke says, "I've never seen such devotion in a droid before."

② THE PIT DROIDS' PERFORMANCE (*THE PHANTOM MENACE*, 1999)

I've always enjoyed seeing robots slightly deviate from their programming, which happens to perfection in *The Phantom Menace*. It occurs when all the podracers are assembling at the starting line for the Boonta Eve Classic and you see three pit droids perfectly acting out a scene that is very reminiscent of The Three Stooges. Simply a pure slice of comedy! Whether it's a protocol droid in *Star Wars* or a bending robot in *Futurama*, it's great to see them skirt the boundaries of their character to provide comic relief.

3 PROBE DROID ON PATROL (*THE EMPIRE STRIKES BACK*, 1980)

The scene on Hoth when you first see the probe droid emerging from the crater is great. Its unique insectile head, spider-like eyes, mechanical mid-section, and long legs give it a very scary and menacing appearance. The probe droid carries on the tradition of terrifying mechanical abominations, which includes the IT-O interrogator droid from *A New Hope* (keen observers will notice it features an R2-D2-style dome). However, the probe droid is markedly improved and a bigger threat thanks to its sensors and unknown weapons system.

4 OOM-SERIES BATTLE DROIDS (*THE PHANTOM MENACE*, 1999)

Like the pit droids, I find the battle droids fascinating and love every scene they are in. Their sole purpose is to obey instructions beamed down from the mothership; they have no intelligence whatsoever. I have two favorite scenes. The first one is the build up to the Battle of Naboo when the battle droids are offloaded from the carrier and expand in unison to form multiple ranks of soldiers. The second is when we are first introduced to the battle droids, as Qui-Gon Jinn and Obi-Wan Kenobi fight their way off the Trade Federation flagship.

5 IMPERIAL SENTRY DROIDS (*THE FORCE AWAKENS*, 2015)

These droids, which I made, are only seen during the Star Destroyer hangar scenes; but it was very fulfilling to see them in the final film, especially as they reflect off the Imperial flight desk with all the explosions going off! I created a prototype first, which was based off concept sketches from Luke Fisher. After it was approved, I made the other two. They were originally supposed to be a mottled gray color, similar to a Star Destroyer, but this was changed to a high gloss to match the stormtroopers.

Interview by Mark Newbold

STAR WARS

INSIDER

®

A HERO'S TALE

Why Luke's Journey Is the Heart of The Saga!

THE FORCE AWAKENS
Teaser Trailer Reaction Inside!

GETTING ANIMATED

CREATING THE CHARACTERS OF STAR WARS REBELS

TITAN

ISSUE #155
US $7.99
CAN $9.99
MARCH 2015

THE CIRCLE IS NOW COMPLETE

RING THEORY

ISSUE 155

MARCH 2015

Lots of people have theories about what the *Star Wars* saga actually means. Some connect it to politics, others see parallels to the Vietnam War, and some, like Mike Klimo, look beyond that to a bigger picture—a *much* bigger picture! I'm not sure I entirely believe Mike's thesis, but that doesn't stop it being a fascinating reading of George Lucas's original saga. His *Insider* feature certainly generated lots of correspondence from readers. What do you think of his 'circular logic'?—**Jonathan Wilkins**

Servants of the Empire: Rebel in the Ranks released

Heir to the Jedi released

Marvel Comics' *Star Wars: Princess Leia* mini-series launches

The Empire Strikes Back Read-Along Storybook and CD released

Marvel Comics' *Star Wars #3: Skywalker Strikes, Part 3* released

Marvel Comics' *Darth Vader #3: Vader, Part 3* released

Star Wars Rebels: Recon Missions released

Honor Among Thieves paperback released

Hera's Phantom Flight released

C-3PO's eye pops in and, later, out again!

THE CIRCLE IS

STAR WARS SCHOLAR MIKE KLIMO ADVOCATES A PATTERNED "RING THEORY" THAT FORMS THE STRUCTURE OF THE *STAR WARS* SAGA. HERE, HE EXPLAINS HIS INTRIGUING IDEA.
INTERVIEW: JONATHAN WILKINS

> "THE INTERESTING THING ABOUT *STAR WARS*—AND I DIDN'T EVER REALLY PUSH THIS VERY FAR, BECAUSE IT'S NOT REALLY THAT IMPORTANT—BUT THERE'S A LOT GOING ON THERE THAT MOST PEOPLE HAVEN'T COME TO GRIPS WITH YET. BUT WHEN THEY DO, THEY WILL FIND IT'S A MUCH MORE INTRICATELY MADE CLOCK THAN MOST PEOPLE WOULD IMAGINE."
> —GEORGE LUCAS, *VANITY FAIR*, FEBRUARY 2005

NOW COMPLETE

A hooded figure revives an "apprentice."

WARS

Star Wars Insider: How did you come to study the *Star Wars* saga so closely?

Mike Klimo: I was born in 1977, twelve days before the release of the film, so I really can't remember a time in my life without *Star Wars*. Like most fans, I've always followed the films pretty closely. But for the longest time, closely meant something more like I can name all of the original members of The Max Rebo Band.

It wasn't until college that I began to analyze the films more critically. I think it had a lot to do with the fact that I kind of walked away from the films for a while and actually learned about things other than *Star Wars*. History, politics, mythology, science, storytelling, and cinema—especially visual literacy, you know, how to read a film and understand the vocabulary of the medium. Plus, I was really starting to watch all different kinds of movies from all over the world. So, when I went back to *Star Wars* it was a lot like returning home after you've traveled abroad for the first time. My perspective on the films was completely changed. Really, up until then, I had no idea that so much was going on under the hood.

Can you talk through the theory and how it works?

Well, this might get a little confusing, so please just stay with me here for a minute. First, I think you have to start with a figure of speech known as "chiasmus." Now, in chiasmus, key words or phrases are repeated in two sentences,

Anakin and Luke leave their loved ones to face their destinies.

"MY PERSPECTIVE ON THE *STAR WARS* FILMS WAS COMPLETELY CHANGED. I HAD NO IDEA THAT SO MUCH WAS GOING ON UNDER THE HOOD."

---

but in reverse order. For example, John F. Kennedy's famous line, "Ask not what your country can do for you, ask what you can do for your country." The second part is a

reversal of the first. So, the words are arranged in an ABB'A' fashion: country(A) you(B) you(B') country(A'). I imagine some of your readers familiar with this concept will point out that technically this is called antimetabole. But for simplicity's sake, let's just say they mean the same thing.

Now, ring composition is really just a larger, more complex version of chiasmus. The story's organized into a sequence of elements that go from a beginning to a well-marked midpoint. Then, the ring turns and the first sequence of elements is repeated *in reverse order* until the story returns to the starting point. That means the first and last elements correspond to each other, the second and second-to-last elements correspond to each other, the third and third-to-last elements correspond to each other, and so on. This creates a sort of circle or mirror image. If we give each element a letter, the pattern is ABC C'B'A', (similar to the JFK example).

And that pattern describes what happens with Episodes I through VI. *The Phantom Menace* (A) corresponds to *Return of the Jedi* (A'); *Attack of the Clones* (B) corresponds to *The Empire Strikes Back* (B'); and *Revenge of the Sith* (C) corresponds to *A New Hope* (C').

What this means is that the sequence of elements (or episodes) starts with

Swooping in from above.

Swinging a lightsaber.

Calm after a traumatic confrontation.

A Jedi enters negotiations.

The Phantom Menace and progresses to *Revenge of the Sith*, where events come to a crucial midpoint. Then, the ring turns and the first sequence (ABC) is repeated in reverse order (C'B'A'), bringing the story full circle back to the beginning.

And whereas corresponding sections in a ring composition are usually marked using key words, each pair of corresponding films in the *Star Wars* ring is meticulously matched using all the different aspects of cinema—including narrative structure, plot points, visuals, dialogue, themes, and music.

Now there's a lot more to it than this, but this will give you the basic idea of the overall pattern. George Lucas has a lot of amazing tricks up his sleeve and takes the idea much, much further. When all is said and done, the six movies actually fit together kind of like puzzle pieces—and they form an image that brings significant meaning to the saga. And in my *Star Wars* Ring Theory essay, I try to walk readers through the whole thing, step-by-step, and make it as easy to understand as possible. But it really is mind-boggling to think about how much time and effort actually went into this.

Are there other examples of ring composition in other media?
Ring composition is a very old technique that's found in a lot of ancient texts from all over the world, from the epic poetry of Homer to the Bible. To the best of my knowledge though, nothing like this has ever been attempted before in cinema. It's just incredible. But in my research for the essay, I did discover a few more

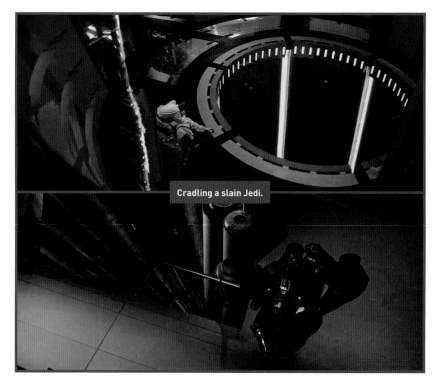

Cradling a slain Jedi.

"WHEN ALL IS SAID AND DONE, THE SIX MOVIES ACTUALLY FIT TOGETHER LIKE PUZZLE PIECES."

modern examples. A one-woman act known as Glasser put out an album in 2010 called *Ring* that was inspired by the idea. And that was really amazing to listen to. But there was one really big example

that I learned about that really blew my socks off. I don't want to give it away here. I think it'd be more fun if readers just Google "John Granger Ring Composition."

Why do you think some people might be surprised to see *Star Wars* taken apart on an academic level?
I don't know. I think some people forget, or don't know, where George Lucas came from. I mean, he came out of San Francisco's avant-garde scene in the 1960s. He was making some really experimental films. So, a lot of people don't realize that *Star Wars* very much reflects those same avant-garde sensibilities. *Star Wars* is not just another Hollywood summer blockbuster made by a committee or marketing department. I really don't think it ever has been. And there's a lot going on in those films that a lot of people are unaware of. Or just assume isn't there because on its surface it looks like something that shouldn't be taken too seriously. But I assure you, nothing could be further from the truth. *Star Wars* deserves the same, if not more, critical attention as any film by Terrence Malick or Wong Kar-Wai. With that being said, there is a lot of more academically minded stuff out there on *Star Wars* in general and the prequels in particular. Probably more so than there's ever been.

Distracted by food!

A stolen kiss.

Yoda reacts to a disturbance.

You just have to do a little work to find it. Because a lot of the time, it gets drowned out by the people with the biggest megaphones—on that wretched hive of scum and villainy known as the Internet. But to me, Anne Lancashire, a Professor at the University of Toronto, is the gold standard. I think her writings on *Empire*, *Jedi*, *The Phantom Menace*, and *Attack of the Clones* should be required reading for anyone studying cinema. And Paul F. McDonald wrote a fantastic book called *The Star Wars Heresies: Interpreting the Themes, Symbols and Philosophies of Episodes I, II, and III.*

Do you think that J.J. Abrams will continue the idea?
I have no idea. Has Lucas even told anyone, or is he keeping this one all to himself? At the end of the day, though, I'm not sure it matters. Personally, I'd much rather see Abrams use *Star Wars* the same way that Lucas did, to express his own unique, uncompromising vision. I look at Episode VII as Abrams' movie. And I can't wait to go on the journey and see where he takes me. And if that journey happens to include ring composition, great. If not, that's okay, too. Either way, I think it's going to be great. Just as long as there are lightsabers. Lots and lots of lightsabers! ☮

MORE TO SAY

Read Mike Klimo's full essay at www.starwarsringtheory.com

HAVE YOU?

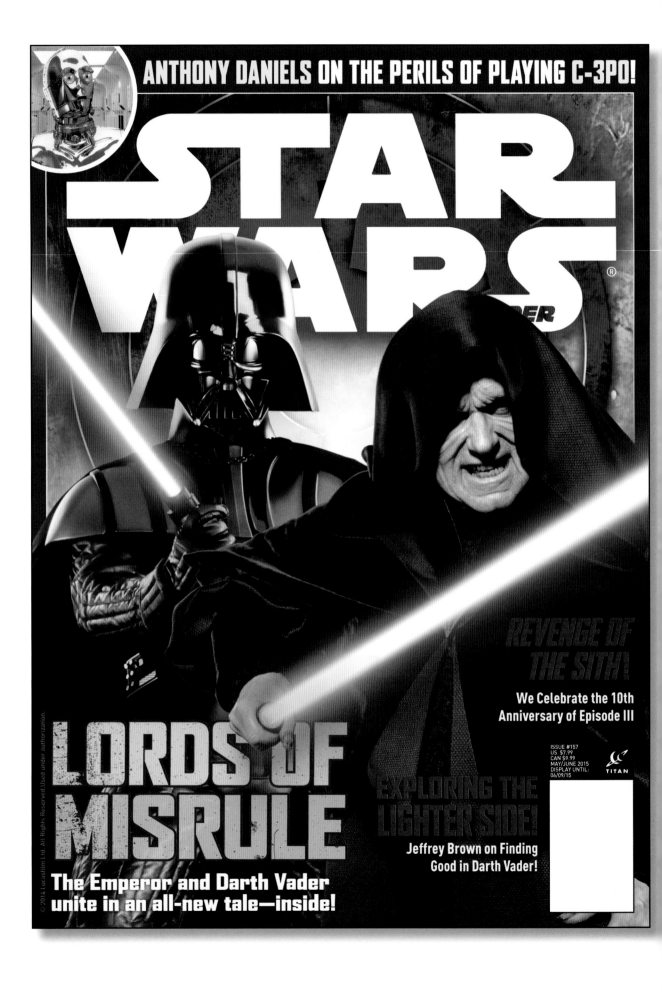

ANTHONY DANIELS ON THE PERILS OF PLAYING C-3PO!

STAR WARS

® INSIDER

REVENGE OF THE SITH!

We Celebrate the 10th Anniversary of Episode III

ISSUE #157
US $7.99
CAN $9.99
MAY/JUNE 2015
DISPLAY UNTIL:
06/09/15

Titan

LORDS OF MISRULE

The Emperor and Darth Vader unite in an all-new tale—inside!

EXPLORING THE LIGHTER SIDE!

Jeffrey Brown on Finding Good in Darth Vader!

C-3PO
ANTHONY DANIELS

ISSUE 157
MAY/JUNE 2015

Star Wars: The Original Marvel Years Volume 2 released

Battle to the End released

Kanan #3: The Last Padawan, Part 3: Pivot released

Although I'm not sure he would agree, C-3PO is surely one of the *Star Wars* saga's biggest icons. The timid, golden droid spends all his time hoping for the quite life, while actually finding himself in the heart of the action. Far more willing to put himself in the thick of things is Anthony Daniels, the actor who has portrayed C-3PO for more than 40 years. Daniels is often to be found at *Star Wars* events around the world, a dedicated ambassador for the saga, and always a gracious host, happy to talk to fans and press alike.
When this interview was conducted, he was fresh off of the set of *The Force Awakens*, helping to promote an exhibition showcasing the power of costumes in the *Star Wars* saga.—**Jonathan Wilkins**

Anthony Daniels was born on February 21, 1946 in Salisbury in the UK. He studied law for two years, before joining the National Theatre of Great Britain at The Young Vic. A meeting with George Lucas led to Daniels accepting the part of C-3PO, the prissy droid who would be a pivotal character throughout the entire Star Wars saga.

CONVERSATION WITH C-3PO

ACTOR ANTHONY DANIELS SPEAKS OUT DURING THE LAUNCH OF THE REBEL, JEDI, PRINCESS, QUEEN: *STAR WARS* AND THE POWER OF COSTUME EXHIBIT. WORDS: TRICIA BARR

The day before the public opening at the EMP Museum in Seattle, I thought it couldn't get any better than a private tour of the new exhibit by the project director. Then the head of Smithsonian Public Relations cut in to reveal that Anthony Daniels had some time to share his thoughts on the exhibit and the iconic costume he brought to life. A minute later we were taking our places in a set of chairs placed conveniently in front of the Droid Design section, C-3PO and R2-D2 gleaming with their pre-opening shine.

A gracious gentleman, Daniels waits until I am seated and needs no prompting to share his thoughts. "I've had lots and lots of experiences beyond the movies because of *him*," he says, gesturing to C-3PO. "I came in from England last night, and came here just after I landed, and I was *really* surprised. I have been to a lot of museum openings, especially the Science and Imagination up in Boston,

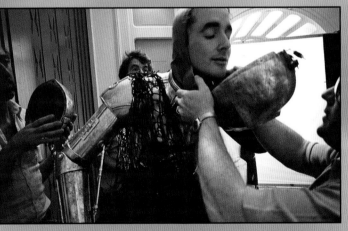

and there's something about the setup here. It starts off with the fact that there are very few plexiglass screens between you and the fabric of the costumes. Even though you can't get near them, I feel you can mentally touch them. It's quite new. There's an innocence about this exhibit. It makes it all seem very real."

For the interview, Daniels faces the display with Padmé's wedding gown. He glances in its direction when he marvels about, "how the costumes were made. How they were knitted together. I just

watched this pearl-stamping machine; I didn't know they did that. It shows just what went into that costume that maybe whisked by in a matter of moments on film. It looked very good but you didn't understand what had gone into it. This exhibit really does honor all the artists who did the embroidery, the gold work, and all that kind of thing.

"What I like about being invited here, for me it's a crossover when I speak to the audience tonight. It's a crossover between the screen of the movie, which is just a piece of white sheet bouncing light back at you, almost taking us into theater, where there is a live person and there is a live audience. The whole thing becomes vivacious, in the sense of being alive. I mean, film's great, but though you may not realize it the actors aren't there at the time, that's just light moving. Whereas here, you get the sense that real people made that film, and that makes the film real."

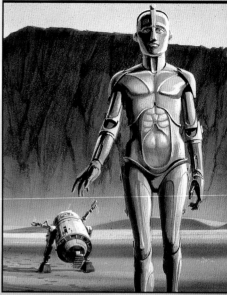

Clockwise, from left: C-3PO aboard the Death Star; the original painting by Ralph McQuarrie that convinced Daniels that the role was worth taking; Chewbacca, R2-D2 and C-3PO; C-3PO as seen in *Attack of the Clones*; having fun with Carrie Fisher on the set of *The Empire Strikes Back*; the droids make their escape from the *Tantive IV*.

IN CONCERT

Daniels compares this experience to another project he participated in. "*Star Wars* in Concert is the best job I ever had. Because it was the films, which is great, but it was with a live audience. And from there you get this strange—you could call it the Force—sense of human togetherness, a collectivness you don't get on a film set. I loved it partly for that, and partly because those thousands of people every night educated me. I could see quite a few rows ahead of me, and hear everybody and sense everybody. It educated me in the sense that I'd never particularly been a *Star Wars* fan; I mean, I'm in them, it slightly robs it of its thrill factor. But what I did get from *Star Wars* in Concert is that millions of people bond with it, millions of people find something in it that I never found.

"I met quite a few fans because of it, and again it educated me, as it does when I come to a convention sometimes; I don't do many. So many people come up and say, 'Thank you for all those years. Thank you for giving me great experiences with my father, he's not here anymore and this makes me think about him.' And that gives a seemingly ridiculous space film far greater value, weight, merit, than just being a film." I comment that he seems to be talking about a kind of family. He

replies, "For some people it was a surrogate family, a safety family. It became a safe haven for quite a few people I've talked to. And therefore when I come to do an event, I do try and retain that respect for it. I don't want to mar anyone's memory. It would almost be sacrilege to hurt it." While Daniels has an amazing grasp

> "I WAS CAPTIVATED BY RALPH MCQUARRIE'S DRAWING. I'VE NEVER BEEN STRUCK QUITE SO MUCH BY AN IMAGE."

on the fandom, I have to ask for his take on C-3PO with the shining costume standing right beside us. "Ralph McQuarrie's drawing—I've told that story so many times, of being captivated by the face in that picture. I've never been struck quite so much by an image. Truly I looked into that face and he looked right back at me." His excitement dims for a moment as he remembers Liz Moore. "This absolutely gorgeous young woman who just was a delight, worked with me molding the plastic cast. She created everything that you see [in the C-3PO on display]. And then she was killed in a car crash before we really began filming. So she never saw Threepio come to life. Yet it was she who created the face. One of the interesting things about the face is, you and I have asymmetrical

faces—so does Threepio. He's not symmetric. You would think you would have a machine that was. But it's subtly different, and it gives you a hint of humanity."

Having gone to drama school and done mime and mask work, Daniels understood the challenges of performing as C-3PO. "A lot comes from hands and such, it's all classic stuff. That pose, partly it's because there's a bridge under my arm so that they can't go down this far." At this point Daniels stands up and affects the protocol droid's wide-elbow stance.

"Partly it's for the center of gravity, because if I'm moving fast, I'm very, very top heavy." Daniels backs away from his chair and continues, "I met the guy who created Robby the Robot, a Japanese gentleman, who told me over breakfast that he didn't like the way his character moved. Because, if you watch him—and he was the first that ever got what I do—Robby walks like this." Daniels lumbers toward me, demonstrating the wide, straight-legged waddle of the *Forbidden Planet* robot. "It's a totally different character, isn't it? If you have this—" he slips effortlessly into the C-3PO shuffle "—it's very unthreatening. He's not a threatening character. I thought a lot about it."

WRONG PLACE, WRONG TIME

While the costume helped define his characterization, the veteran actor also shares insight on C-3PO's role in the saga. "Very clearly he was always in the wrong place, and it was always the wrong time. He was totally unskilled in anything useful in the storyline. He was skilled in things nobody ever wanted him to do. That leads to a certain amount of frustration. Especially given the skills in his case—gentle and social and societal—and he was never asked to do this. He was always running away from explosions, something completely alien to him. This gives you a great dramatic contrast."

Sitting among all those amazing costumes, I can't resist the chance to ask Daniels to choose his favorite costume. Without hesitation he responds, "Anything you can sit down in." Given the scope and detail of the prequel trilogy films, I ask him about Padmé's dresses. "Palpatine thought he had more frock, but I'm not sure. I'd have to say slightly, perhaps I took them for granted. It just seemed so normal at the time. It's only somewhere like this that you can actually come up and stare. You don't

have to be somebody who knits or sews or embroiders to say, 'Wow, that's pretty good, the man-hours, woman-hours, people-hours that have gone into these things. You don't see the detail in the film.

"An exhibition like this allows you to be amazed that there are people on this planet—and apparently other planets in other galaxies—who can do this stuff. Now there are not many people who can afford this kind of thing, because it costs

"SEE-THREEPIO WAS UNSKILLED IN ANYTHING USEFUL IN THE STORYLINE!"

a lot of money. I'm always commenting that in days past it was the church, it was monarchs, who could pay for this kind of thing. Patrons of the arts. In many ways the film industry allows these arts to exist, and hopefully increase. With the money that comes from videogames now, you can pay people to do amazing things."

This leads to me to ask if George Lucas is a patron of the arts, too. "Hugely. Because of his work, his investment in it, he's allowed these arts to flourish. One of the things I absolutely admire about *Star Wars* is that it's encouraged people—kids

and grown-ups—to be creative. Don't buy a stormtrooper costume; just make one. It has to be the spirit of a stormtrooper. It doesn't have to be totally shiny; use cardboard. Anybody who's here today in a costume that they made, they get a hug—even if they don't want one. I've met so many people who are scientists and roboticists, musicians, painters, designers, teachers, because of *Star Wars*.

"I teach at Carnegie Mellon University at the Entertainment Technology Center. It is amazing if you tease out of the students the facts that they remember about *Star Wars*, the saga; you find in there a complete paradigm of any story. And you can take from it the creation of the icon. In this room there are several iconic images, and that means something that anybody would recognize, anywhere in the world. C-3PO, of course, being one of them. Darth Vader is upstairs. R2-D2. Chewbacca is there. These are icons. People don't realize that when they see them. They just say, 'I know him.' That's the thing about an icon. It speaks more about being just a gold metal suit. You suddenly put Threepio in context, and you think, *Yeah, he did this and this and he met so-and-so.*"

Right: Behind the scenes on the *Tantive IV* (Daniels is on the left).

Opposite page: On the set of *The Empire Strikes Back* with John Hollis (Lobot); an uncharacteristically dynamic pose from our favorite protocol droid; C-3PO and Luke; behind-the-scenes on the Jabba's palace set.

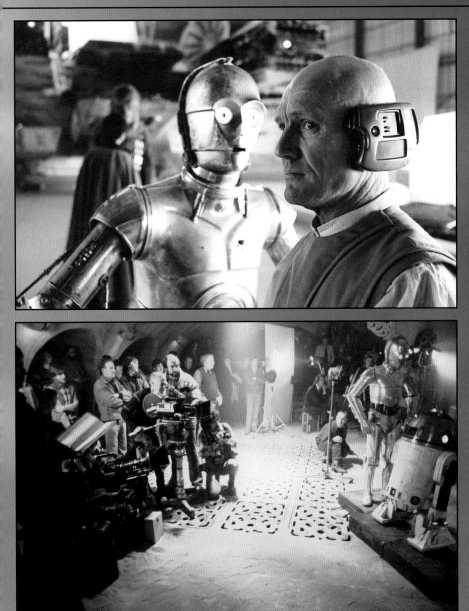

INTO THE FUTURE

Thoroughly jazzed by Daniels' enthusiasm for the upcoming movie, I take a second to remember the final question on my list. It's not another role in a movie, but writing the foreword to the book *Ultimate Star Wars*, due to be released on April 28. Daniels seems a little perplexed how I know about his participation— until I explain that I'm one of the encyclopedia's four authors. Daniels smiles. "DK are a terrific company. To be asked to write the foreword to *Ultimate Star Wars* was quite an honor, because I'm just one of the things that goes in to making the finished picture. There are lots of people involved."

That admission turns Daniels a bit reflective on *Star Wars*' place in history. "If you think that people are still being taught Homer's *Odyssey* or whatever in school, and how many thousand years ago was that? Two thousand years ago? So there's no reason why people in that age, a thousand years from now, won't be learning about *Star Wars*. Because actually, George has just taken that and moved it into a default. And that was his clever thing, to take this familiarity, so we felt at home." ✪

STAR WARS®

REBEL ROUSER
Ahsoka Tano takes the Hero's Journey!

CAPTAIN FANTASTIC
Actor Dee Bradley Baker on the return of Rex!

RETURNING TO JEDI
SECRETS OF THE CLASSIC NOVEL!

ISSUE 160
OCT 2015
U.S. $7.99
Can $9.99

TITAN

INSIDE:

JOURNEY TO **STAR WARS**: THE FORCE AWAKENS

WHAT NEXT FOR OUR HEROES?

ALIENS
STRANGE CREATURES FROM ANOTHER GALAXY

ISSUE 160
OCTOBER 2015

The original trailer for *Star Wars* boasted that audiences would see "aliens from a thousand worlds." It's a lovely bit of exaggeration of the kind that you are only allowed to do in trailers. Somebody who was really taking notice was Tom Spina, who saw *Star Wars* when he was a child and was inspired enough to become a professional creature restorer. His knowledge of the monsters and aliens is absolute, so he was the perfect choice to nominate some iconic aliens that will probably inspire further generations to take an interest in this fascinating field.—**Jonathan Wilkins**

TOM SPINA'S FIVE FAVORITE ALIENS!

AS A BOY, TOM SPINA WAS SO INSPIRED BY THE CANTINA SEQUENCE IN THE ORIGINAL *STAR WARS*, THAT HE ENDED UP FOUNDING A COMPANY THAT SPECIALIZES IN RESTORING MOVIE MONSTERS!

1 THE CANTINA BAND

Ever since I first opened up the *Star Wars Storybook* and saw the spread of Cantina monsters, the band has really symbolized the *Star Wars* alien look for me. Rick Baker's vision and Doug Beswick's sculpting (along with paint by the late Laine Liska) combined to create a classic species—one that was made all the better by the fact that there were seven of them!

COOL FACTOR: Don Post's wonderful rubber masks of these guys!

BONUS COOL FACTOR: Recently discovered images and sketches show they'd originally intended for the species to have a second mouth... on its neck! The additional instrument hole was abandoned prior to making the masks for the film.

2 NIKTO

I've always loved the ruddy coloration and the wonderful lines of the sculpture. I absolutely love the way the nostrils trace their way around the mouth and create a "nose" that vents out near his chin; all wonderful design, paint, and character work. They did a great job recreating this one for the prequels as well.

COOL FACTOR: His name is taken from one of my favorite movies: *The Day the Earth Stood Still*.

BONUS COOL FACTOR: Each of these guys in *Return of the Jedi* got their own style of awesome headgear!

KENNER'S BLUE SNAGGLETOOTH

I got my first *Star Wars* figures for Christmas and Kenner's Snaggletooth was my favorite from the start! It was a unique interpretation of one of Stuart Freeborn's team's somewhat "earthbound" aliens. He always looked a bit bovine to me, but with his Kiss style silver boots and rockin' belt buckle, he pulled it off.

COOL FACTOR: The belt buckle was added by the figure's sculptor, who used his own business card logo as inspiration.
BONUS COOL FACTOR: The *Star Wars Holiday Special* then copied that logo on the belt of its incarnation of the character, who was then copied by Kenner for its shorter, red Snaggletooth figure!

JABBA THE HUTT

My folks recorded *From Star Wars to Jedi: The Making of a Saga* when it aired on PBS, and I must've just about worn through that poor VHS tape! I already loved the Cantina and watching Phil Tippett's crew create the aliens for Jabba's palace was inspiring beyond words, but seeing the effort put into creating and puppeteering Jabba was truly special. That they built this giant foam beast was incredible. That it worked so well and was as believable as the humans and costumed aliens he was acting with is a real tribute to the artistry of all involved!

HORRENDOUS CREATURE

BONUS ALIEN: Jabba's palace alien, Hermi Odle, whose disgusting look I loved instantly when I got the Topps blue series card simply titled, "Horrendous creature!"

DEWBACK

I don't know if this is an alien or a creature, but since we don't have them on Earth, I'm calling it an alien. There's an image of the dewback and sandtrooper that graced the pages of the original 1977 souvenir program that, to me, summarizes *Star Wars* more than any other image. This wondrous combination of a skull-faced, high-tech soldier riding what looks like a dinosaur, each weathered and loaded with gear, just epitomizes the vibe and feel of the films I love.
COOL FACTOR: The dewback's head and tail were sculpted pieces, but the body is actually a taxidermy form for a rhinoceros!

Interview by Mark Newbold

FIRST LOOK AT DISNEY'S NEW INDIANA JONES ADVENTURE!

NEW DORMAN ART—
MAGISTRATES OF
THE EMPIRE

STAR WARS INSIDER

ISSUE #25
$3.50-U.S., $4.00-CAN.

THE DROID vs. THE DARK LORD
ANTHONY DANIELS AND JAMES EARL JONES GO ONE-ON-ONE WITH THE INSIDER

PLUS

A REPORT FROM TOY FAIR

PREQUEL UPDATE WITH RICK McCALLUM

STAR WARS NEWS FROM AROUND THE GLOBE!

VADER'S VOICE
JAMES EARL JONES

ISSUE 25
SPRING 1995

Ambush at Corellia released

Classic Star Wars: The Early Adventures #8 released

Tales of the Jedi: Dark Lords of the Sith #6: *Jedi Assault* released

Burl Ives, the narrator of *Caravan of Courage: An Ewok Adventure*, dies

Dark Empire II #5: *The Galaxy Weapon* released

Children of the Jedi released

Dark Empire II #6: *Hand of Darkness* released

Providing *Star Wars* with its most distinctive voice, James Earl Jones' performance as Darth Vader is as iconic as it gets. Another actor, David Prowse, embodied Vader's physical presence, and Jones has always been modest enough to downplay his own contribution. But his modulated voice is key to Darth Vader's impact and timeless appeal, creating a perfect marriage of sound and vision.

Personally, I think this is partly down to the fact that everybody thinks they can do the Vader voice, and I've yet to meet anybody who won't at least try! But nobody else sounds quite like Vader, and Jones' performance takes a great script and injects it with a powerful mix of passion and menace that defines the dark lord. This is best exemplified in *The Empire Strikes Back*, where—realizing the high stakes for the character—Jones turns things up a notch, vocalizing a sense of single-minded desperation.**—Jonathan Wilkins**

James Earl Jones was born on January 17, 1931 in Arkabutla, Mississippi. He made his Broadway debut in 1957 and—over the course of a career spanning more than 60 years—has become one of the most loved and respected actors in the USA. He has won many accolades, including Tony and Golden Globe Awards for his role in The Great White Hope *on Broadway, and three Emmys for his TV work. He was also nominated for the Academy Award for Best Actor in the film adaptation of* The Great White Hope *(1970). He first voiced Darth Vader in 1977, and went on to win a whole new legion of fans with another iconic vocal role in 1994, when he played Mufasa in Disney's* The Lion King. *Today, he continues to provide the voice of Darth Vader, most recently in* Star Wars Rebels *and* Rogue One: A Star Wars Story.

speaking for DARTH

the magic of James Earl Jones

by Pete Hull

Throughout the ages, armies of weary soldiers have sought refuge in the magic of words.

For a moment, the day's losses are forgotten. For a moment, the moans of the wounded and the terrible smell of death are forgotten. Tomorrow they will face death again. But for now, a solitary figure is silhouetted against the campfire commanding their full attention.

He practices an art borne many millennia before the sound byte. Tonight, in the earliest tradition of the theater, he will fill them with courage and ease their pain. He is the storyteller, a magician of words and imagery.

Today, actors are these modern-day magicians and you have heard one of the best.

As you sat in the dark of the theater, watching the ultimate contest of good versus evil, you didn't see him. You only heard him.

James Earl Jones may be the last of a tradition. Because of technology none like him may ever follow again. Today children sit in front of the television and learn from distant magicians. But not so with James Earl Jones. He learned his craft in the oral tradition—through stories passed down from father and mother to sons and daughters.

"Papa used to tell me my child-voice was beautiful, like a bell," James Earl wrote in his autobiography *Voices and Silence*.

"I grew up listening to the music of Southern voices, the rich oral testimonies guised in stories told on the porch at Papa's or at my great grandfather's home. The storytellers in the family could mesmerize us with the high drama of our family tales or with local vivid gossip. At night, I listened with fascination and sometimes fear to Mama's epic bedtime stories. Out in the country, with few books or strangers, and no such thing as television, we depended on the stories we knew, and the stories we could invent and tell ourselves. I grew up with the spoken word."

But James Earl—that's what he asked us to call him—has a special relationship to words. His voice didn't always come easily to him. When he was young, he stuttered.

"If you are denied an ability, or if you suffer from an inability to express yourself," he told us, "expression becomes a very important thing. You appreciate those people who can express themselves."

When he was a young boy, James Earl developed a stutter after his family moved from Mississippi to Michigan. Those early childhood days were difficult for him. James Earl was shy and the stutter only made things worse. He withdrew into silence.

"Professor Donald Crouch, a high school teacher in English, history and Latin, inspired me to overcome my stuttering," he tells us.

"First of all, he acknowledged that there were certain situations where I didn't stutter, One was when I talked to animals on the farm. The other was when I read my own poetry So, he just encouraged me to write more poetry and recite it in front of the class.

"Many people who eventually achieve something, those people whom we know of for their accomplishments, start out with a handicap. Had they not overcome that handicap, it would have denied them the opportunity to do what they did. But they did overcome it, and they become better for it."

James Earl adds, "It's not unusual and I don't make a lot of it (stuttering). It's just that in my own life and in my own work, I'm happy when the words come out right."

James Earl stepped onto the stage in 1950, and since then the words have "come out right" in more than 66 theater productions, 51 movies and 28 television shows or made-for-television movies. He cast his spell in movies such as *Matewan*, *Gardens of Stone*, *Coming to America*, *Field of Dreams*, *The Hunt for Red October*, *Patriot Games*, *Sommersby* and *Clear and Present Danger*. Additionally, the rich resonance of his voice became the voice of Mufasa, the father lion in *The Lion King*. And around the world, it is his voice that announces "This is CNN," just before the cable network takes a station break.

On stage, in the movies and on television, James Earl has played an amazing variety of characters. In both the play and the movie *The Great White Hope*, he played Jack Johnson, the first African-American heavyweight boxing champion. In *Field of Dreams*, he co-starred with Kevin Costner as a famous writer. (By the way, James Earl says that people who have seen *Field of Dreams* believe they recall the character he portrays from their memories of the 60s. But the character is fictional, there never was an activist-writer named Terrence Mann.) And in *The Vernon Johns Story*, James Earl plays the role of the early civil rights activist.

For these and other powerful performances, James Earl has earned an amazing 37 major awards including three Emmys, two Tonys, a Golden Globe, a Grammy and an Obie. In one year (1991), he won two Emmys for two different performances: one in *Gabriel's Fire* and the other in *Heat Wave*. In 1967-1968, he won his first Tony Award, this one for Best Performance by an Actor, for the play *The Great White Hope*. In 1970, *The Great White Hope* went to the silver screen and James Earl received his first Academy Award nomination—Best Performance by an Actor. He won his second Tony Award in 1987 for the play *Fences*.

James Earl's list of awards seems endless. But surprisingly, it doesn't include any awards for his performances in the *Star Wars* trilogy

"I was once a member of the Board of Directors of the Academy of Motion Picture Arts and Sciences and we had to acknowledge that a film's success reflects, in ways, its excellence. *Star Wars* was successful, yet it didn't get a lot of awards. I'm not saying a successful movie should be given artistic credit just because it's successful. But there's something right that happened about that movie that made it successful. That should be recognized."

Even though *Star Wars* didn't earn James Earl much recognition from his industry peers, it changed his life.

"It set off a chain reaction of voices in my career. With Darth Vader, my voice came to be used more and more frequently as a voice of authority. It brought me a lot of commercial and voice-over work." James Earl and Penelope Niven wrote in his autobiography: "The voice-over work led to more and more opportunities for narrations and on-camera commercials, with their milieu and craft so different from movies and theater."

Before it became widely known that James Earl was the voice of Darth Vader, he used to deny it. "It was fun," he says in his book. "I used to tell people that the film's producers first called up Orson Welles, and he was busy, so they called up Victor Jury, and he was busy, so they called me."

We asked him to tell us more about that story.

"After he put the film together, George Lucas decided that he wanted a voice in the bass register. I don't think that David Prowse is a bass. David also has a slight Scottish accent. So, George began to look for someone to do a voice-over.

"I understand that George did contact several actors to read for the voice of Darth Vader before he contacted me. I was out of work and he said 'do you want a day's work?' and I said 'sure.'"

"DAVID PROWSE WORKED VERY HARD TO CREATE THE CHARACTER DARTH VADER. HE IS VADER.
I JUST CONSIDER MYSELF TO BE SPECIAL EFFECTS."

James Earl has fond memories of doing the movies. "They were all a joy." he says, then pauses for a minute, and jokes, "'Cause after all, David Prowse did all the hard work of wearing that hot suit."

He becomes a little more serious for a minute.

"David Prowse worked very hard to create the character Darth Vader. He is Vader. I just consider myself to be special effects. That's how I approached it. I just sat there and had all the fun of playing my voice like an instrument."

The voice of Darth Vader was laid onto the film in a process called looping. Looping is done in a room of the same name—a looping room—by an actor who tries to synchronize his lines with the movements of his lips on-screen. You've seen the effects of bad looping: the actor's mouth is moving and there is no sound. Or there is voice and no mouth movement. And of course, if it was good looping, you wouldn't know it was looped. It looks and sounds natural.

"You usually stand when you are looping. The voice behaves differently when you stand in contrast to when you sit," he explains.

"Even though there was no synchronization problems because Darth's mouth was covered by the mask, George Lucas wanted me to see the character's behavior to give me some clue to his mental and emotional state, or to his lack of emotion. So, I was watching the film as I looped. It only took about two and a half hours to complete the looping for the first film.

"For movies two and three we set aside the whole day - eight hours, for the looping of Vader's voice. In number two, I didn't know quite what we had done right in the first one. As an actor, I wanted to improve my performance. I wanted to do a good job, to be more expressive. But we discovered that being more expressive wasn't the right approach for Vader.

"George Lucas and the others and I sat around and asked the question, 'if you deal with the voice as a musical instrument in terms of human inflection, what is Darth's voice?'"

They discovered it is unique because it is very narrow. "I think one of them said, 'that's probably the mistake we're making. Vader doesn't express himself with his voice. The word is there, he lays it out, and that's it.'"

James Earl explains, "Vader is a man who never learned the beauties and subtleties of human expression. So we figured out the key to my work was to keep it on a very narrow band. A narrow band of expression - that was the secret."

This narrow band of expression made one particular moment all that more powerful.

"Luke, I am your father."

Those five simple words froze armies of audiences in shock and disbelief.

Baseball, Dreams and Life
by Pete Hull

Three of James Earl Jones' works—*The Bingo Long Traveling All-Stars and Motor Kings* (1976), *Fences* (1985) and *Field of Dreams* (1989), are about baseball or baseball players.

That seemed like a lot of stories about the same thing. So we asked the question: Do you have a special tie to that sport?

"No. Not at all," said James Earl Jones.

"We lived in a farming region in Michigan where there was no electricity. We had a car battery hooked up to a radio and that's how we got baseball. But I didn't really learn about baseball until the movie *Bingo Long*.

"It was only then that I learned how to stand at a plate like a batter. And then I became fascinated as to why you couldn't hit the ball, even by accident, unless you saw it as you hit it. I then realized that even though it is a team sport, it relies on a lot of individual acts of heroism."

But James Earl was never an athlete. "The choice I made was to spend time with Professor Donald Crouch learning how to talk. That took me away from the whole area of sports. Although I'm probably built like a football player, I'm not an athlete at all. I did a little track. I was rotten in basketball—no—I was *horrible* in basketball.

"We rarely had a baseball team. It was a small agricultural high school, so I was spared all that. I was spared the obsession with athletic prowess. And I think fortunately for me."

Fortunately as well, James Earl had dreams of being a doctor, not an athlete.

"I went through pre-med at the University of Michigan and then joined the army. The army fascinated me. I loved it, I just loved it. I loved the activity, the being outdoors, the rough and tumble. It was a life that I fit in with very well. I think every kid should have that experience. And I don't think you can be complete unless you develop both sides of yourself."

After discussing sports and all three of his baseball-related projects, we realized that if we wanted a better understanding of James Earl we needed to consider some of his other performances.

Looking into these other projects, we noticed that most of James Earl Jones' works have several layers of meaning. All are great stories as well, yet touch each of us a bit differently.

The play *Fences*, for instance, was not just about a former baseball player whose son has been offered a football scholarship; it's about a man in trouble and a family in trouble.

The same is true with *Gabriel's Fire*. *Gabriel's Fire* is not only about detective or police work or an ex-con; it's about new-found freedom. *The Great White Hope* as well is not just about boxing; it's the complex story of one black man striving to do what black men had never done before.

Finally we considered *Matewan*. This film is based on a true story. In 1920, in the West Virginia town of the same name, 10,000 coal miners battled federal troops and planes deployed by President Warren G. Harding. In the movie, James Earl plays an aging coal miner named Few Clothes. Few Clothes defied the mine bosses to fight for fair treatment of the miners. It is a story about a man who finds the courage to challenge the system.

For 40 years, James Earl has been there like a great hitter, play after play. Sometimes he has hit home runs. Sometimes he has punted. But he has always been a great player—the type that brings the crowd to its feet. The type that makes you forget the troubles of the day for a few moments. The type who can tell a great story.

Hearing James Earl's explanation of Vader's narrow band of expression, it makes that line all the more understandable. Vader's lack of emotion energized this line with incredible power. The lack of feeling in this most emotional of statements by Vader revealed the power of the dark side of the Force.

"I just recall thinking 'Darth Vader is lying,'" says James Earl. "At the time I didn't know for sure."

Will we get to hear James Earl Jones as the voice of some young Darth Vader in upcoming movies?

"No, I don't think so. It's not just Darth's age that makes him sound

131

my way. My voice mattered only once he had become bionic. So, there could conceivably be a short piece after he has fallen into the volcano when you hear my voice. But before the mask is on, Vader is another actor with another voice. Only once the mask is on do I become the voice of Darth Vader "

The Lion King, was a similar kind of experience for James Earl in that it was voice acting. In this movie, James Earl plays the voice of Musafa, the father lion.

"I watched all sorts of National Geographic and Discovery channel coverage of lions. The male lion is lazy. Well he's not actually lazy, he's the king, he doesn't have to hunt."

They made two tracks of his voice. "I think the original Musafa track was very kingly and very unapproachable, so we began to soften him. We made him a Dad too. We made him more... 'dopey I call it."

James Earl went on to extoll the benefits of voice acting. "The interesting thing about voice acting is you don't have to worry about how you look. We could just sort of freak out on sound. With the hyenas, I'm sure that it was great for them to have the freedom not to worry about

"I feel I'm very lucky to have had any association with *Star Wars* because it gave me exposure to another generation," says Jones. "They might not give a hoot about the next thing I do on Broadway, but they did care about *Star Wars*."

who's watching. Just simply make the sound that could make this movie very exciting and very interesting. I think voice acting has become a legitimate kind of category and maybe someday it will be recognized."

This winter, James Earl starred in a powerful television drama, *The Vernon Johns Story*. Many don't know the name Vernon Johns, yet he was one of the founders of the civil rights movement.

Because there's not footage on him (the media had not yet begun to cover the drama of the civil rights movement at that time), James Earl had little guidance when studying for the role. He found only one interesting photograph of Johns at the pulpit.

"I believe in the news. I believe in the news media. And we rely on the news media for a lot of our edification if not our education. I'm one of those who did not know of Vernon Johns. You can't blame the public for not knowing - there was nothing broadcast about him.

"However, there was one audio recording of a sermon that he gave at Howard University chapel. It is called 'The Romance of Death, and I had the opportunity to hear it. It is phenomenal.

"That sermon, just hearing him speak, convinced me to do the part. Even though Vernon John's voice was silenced, he gave us much to be grateful for. After Mr Johns was forced to leave his congregation, a new minister took over his church. His name was Dr Martin Luther King."

It's almost time for us to say good-bye to James Earl. We ask him one last question.

How does he feel about *Star Wars*?

James Earl tells us he is a science fiction fan. "I like science fiction and so therefore I was an immediate and automatic fan. But none of us realized at that time that it would become the phenomenon it did. It was impressive.

"I feel I'm very lucky to have had any association with *Star Wars* because it gave me exposure to another generation. They might not give a hoot about the next thing I do on Broadway, but they did care about *Star Wars*.

"It's like the kids who cared about *The Lion King*. That was a whole different project and a whole new generation of viewers. But for a period of time, I had the chance to perform for them."

And while those children (and adults) who enjoyed *The Lion King* may not have realized it, they were listening to one of the master magicians of our time. ✦

Pete Hull is a freelance writer living in Pebble Beach, Ca.

If you would like to learn more about James Earl Jones, check with your bookstore or library for his book, *Voices and Silence*. It is written by James Earl Jones and Penelope Niven and was published by Macmillian Publishing in 1993.

STAR WARS INSIDER

Samuel L. Jackson
Exclusive Prequel Interview

Billy Dee Williams
Our Man Lando

Episode I
News and Photos

Red Leader Lives!

MATT GROENING

THE Simpsons
STRIKE BACK
STAR WARS ON TV'S MOST POPULAR ANIMATED SHOW

ISSUE 38 U.S.A $4.50 CANADA $5.95

LANDO
BILLY DEE WILLIAMS

ISSUE 38
JUNE/JULY 1998

The Mandalorian Armor released

X-Wing: Iron Fist released

Galaxy of Fear: Clones released

The Essential Guide to Planets and Moons released

Tales of the Jedi: Redemption #1: *A Gathering of Jedi* released

Han Solo may well be the coolest hero in the *Star Wars* saga, but even he could be outcharmed by Lando Calrissian as portrayed by the suave and charismatic Billy Dee Williams. Judging from his convention appearences and the times when I was privileged enough to meet Williams, there is a lot of Cloud City's Baron Administrator in this talented actor, artist, singer, and writer. He's always charming to interview, hugely knowledgeable on numerous topics, especially art (Williams is an accomplished artist himself), and demonstrates a deadpan sense of humor with a twinkle in his eye.

As a bonus, this feature includes a brief but fascinating interview with Lando's usually silent right-hand man, Lobot, otherwise known as John Hollis.**—Jonathan Wilkins**

William December "Billy Dee" Williams Jr. was born on April 6, 1937, in New York. After appearing on Broadway at the age of eight, he found stardom as an adult on the big screen in the likes of The Last Angry Man *(1959),* Nighthawks *(1981), and* Batman *(1989), and on TV in movies such as* Carter's Army *(1970) and* Brian's Song *(1971) . A graduate of the National Academy of Fine Arts and Design in New York, Williams has had his paintings exhibited in the National Portrait Gallery, the Smithsonian, and the Schomburg Center. Most famous for playing Lando Calrissian in* The Empire Strikes Back *and* Return of the Jedi, *he has recently lent his vocal talents to* Star Wars Rebels, Star Wars Battlefront, The LEGO Movie, *and* The LEGO Batman Movie.

Bertie Wyn Hollis (known as John) was born in southwest London in 1927. His numerous screen roles include parts in The Dirty Dozen. *He appeared in the films* Superman *and* Superman II *as an elder of Krypton, and in* Superman IV: The Quest for Peace *as a Russian General. He also played the role of Ernst Stavro Blofeld in the James Bond film* For Your Eyes Only.

an audience with
Billy Dee Williams
Among the Clouds

BY SCOTT CHERNOFF

Billy Dee Williams believes in himself. The super-suave actor, who brought an aura of dashing cool to the *Star Wars* universe as Cloud City's charming rogue Lando Calrissian, has even more self-confidence in real life than he projected in *Return of the Jedi* when he casually boasted, "Someone must have told them about my little maneuver at the battle of Taanab."

In fact, chatting on a recent afternoon with Williams—who also starred in such films as *Batman*, *Brian's Song*, *Nighthawks*, and *Lady Sings the Blues*—it becomes clear that the actor *is* Lando Calrissian. All the charm, bluster, guile, integrity, and complexity that made Calrissian such a classic character comes straight from Billy Dee. So too does Lando's barrier-breaking spirit.

"I have always had a style of my own," Billy Dee told the *Insider*, "but I didn't sit around and figure it out. It's self-esteem—you're not adhering to everybody else's idea of what you should be. You're pretty comfort-

able being a maverick. The idea of being an iconoclast, an eccentric, is something that appeals to me."

That brash individualism has served Billy Dee well throughout a long and diverse career that has encompassed acting, painting, writing—and even at one point the release of Undeniable, his own Avon fragrance.

Undeniable was indeed an apt moniker for Williams' signature scent, since it also summed up the strength of his appeal. In the 1970s and into the '80s, Billy Dee Williams was *the* African-American romantic leading man of cinema—one of the most successful black stars in an era when black leading men were few and far between.

"There are a lot of things I wanted to do on film that I was not able to do because people were not prepared to do them, because of ethnicity," Billy Dee said. "The industry just wouldn't let me do it. The fact that I

Illustration by Hugh Fleming

became the first black romantic hero on the screen was unprecedented. Even then, it was very hard for a lot of people to deal with that—but they couldn't make it go away."

In fact, Billy Dee became so popular that his fame transcended his race, paving the way for a new generation of black actors. Whether he was soaring through space as Lando Calrissian, romancing Diana Ross in *Lady Sings the Blues* and *Mahogany*, or barging into a tavern, clad in a tux, to pitch Colt 45 malt liquor in a legendary series of TV commercials, Billy Dee Williams became known as one of the most dashing and debonair stars in Hollywood.

"I think I have a lasting quality that's like Gable and those guys—no matter how long ago, they'll always be remembered," Billy Dee

>> *When the movie came out, I would pick up my daughter from school, and these kids would run up to me and say, "You betrayed Han Solo!"*

said. "I was also deemed the black Clark Gable. That wasn't even a publicity thing—I would have people run up to me in the supermarket saying, 'I have to tell you this: you are the black Clark Gable.'"

Billy Dee told the *Insider* that he saw his opportunity to join the cast of *The Empire Strikes Back* in 1979 as a key element in his plan to break through racial stereotypes. "Being a hero was a very big part of my thinking at that time," he said, "because I really wanted to create something that nobody seemed to want to look at. I have always somehow seen myself that way, and I wanted to present myself that way. So it worked."

It sure did. Somehow, in *Empire* and *Jedi*, Billy Dee Williams effortlessly achieved the impossible: he crashed the holy trinity of *Star Wars* stars—Mark Hamill, Harrison Ford, and Carrie Fisher—and established himself as the fourth essential member of that heroic team, even though he is nowhere to be seen in the first *Star Wars* adventure.

Looking back on his early days on the *Empire* set in London, Billy Dee confided, "It was difficult because I was the new boy on the block. They were like a little family—and that's

what George creates: he creates a family."

But from his first appearance, greeting Han, Leia, Chewie, and Threepio on the landing platform in Cloud City, Lando commanded audience attention. Fans were intrigued by this caped lothario described by Solo as "a card-player, gambler, scoundrel." His history as the original owner of the *Millennium Falcon*, current status as administrator of the visually dazzling Bespin mining colony Cloud City, and his suave, supercool persona, all served as a seductive cover for Lando's initial betrayal of his old friend. The fact that he was always shadowed by a bald, headphone-wearing cyborg named Lobot didn't hurt his image either.

With lines like, "You truly belong here with us among the clouds" which he smoothly cooed to Princess Leia while kissing her hand upon meeting her, Billy Dee was the perfect choice for the dashing, swashbuckling space entrepreneur. "I could see why they chose me to do it, because I have those qualities," Billy Dee said. "I wanted to make him that kind of a guy."

But even though Lando realized his mistake by the end of *Empire* and helped Leia, Luke, Chewie, and the droids escape from the Bespin system, many fans at first found it difficult to reconcile Lando's charming approach with the way he handed his old buddy Han right over to Darth Vader and Boba Fett, two of the most hardcore villains in the galaxy. It just didn't seem like something a friend would do.

"When the movie came out," Billy Dee recalled, "I would pick up my daughter from school, and these kids would run up to me and say, 'You betrayed Han Solo!' I would then find myself getting into the middle of trying to explain the whole situation. Even airline stewardesses would tell me I betrayed Han Solo. I would say, 'You don't understand—it was a very peculiar situation. I had to deal with Darth Vader, and also I had Cloud City—this is my domain and I didn't want to lose it because these people showed up with Darth Vader on their tail. So I had to figure out how to save them.' Listen to me, I'm doing it now."

Flashing back to the persecution, Billy Dee proceeded to present a spirited defense of the deceptively debonair Calrissian. "He had to save his situation," Billy Dee rationalized. "Lando and

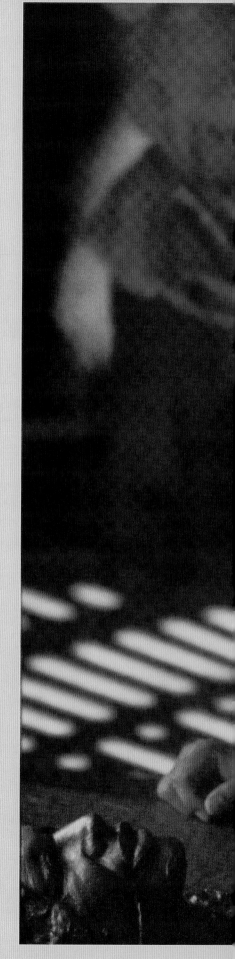

>> **Clockwise: Lando stands over his frozen friend in a tense scene. Billy Dee Williams takes aim at the Empire; a rogue pair, Harrison Ford and Billy Dee Williams.**

Han Solo are pretty much the same kind of people: they're hustlers, and they gamble and figure out ways to do things without too much violence—although I think probably Han Solo is a little bit more on the violent side than Lando, because Lando gets his stuff through charm.

"But," he continued, "I had to do it in such a way that there wouldn't be a complete demise of Han Solo or the rest, but I knew there would have to be some sort of delay." Suddenly, Billy Dee became even more animated, taking on the character of Lando in a sponta-

ics, it's about that farm boy and his growth." Then Billy Dee added, "When I say a lot of this stuff, a lot of times I'm just saying it in jest. You know me—I don't really mean it."

But despite his jovial demeanor, Billy Dee admitted, "I'm not always smiling. I'm a mercurial kind of person. I'm a brooder by nature. But I've always been happy. My mother tells me that when I was little I was always acting out characters and telling jokes all the time. But I always remember being a brooder. I isolate myself so that when I do get out it's really such

artistic atmosphere. Romanticism was still in the air." One day, he said, "I was running around looking for a cigarette, and this producer and director just walked up to me and said, 'Are you an actor?' I said, 'Uh, yeah.' They asked me to come in for an audition."

This time, though, Billy Dee didn't get the part. "I wasn't seasoned enough," he said. "I

>> I'm not always smiling. I'm a mercurial kind of person. I'm a brooder by nature. But I've always been happy.

neously electrifying reprise: "I lost everything," he insisted. "I lost everything because of that whole situation! I even stood up to Darth Vader, which most people don't do. Look at what he did to the guy at the opening of the movie on the ship there!"

Despite Billy Dee's impassioned protestations to schoolchildren and airline stewardesses, the jury remained out on Lando until he returned for *Return of the Jedi* as a general in the Rebel Alliance, leading the attack on the Death Star while riding shotgun in the *Millennium Falcon* with his own jolly Sullustan sidekick, Nien Nunb, laughing all the way. Suddenly, all was forgiven.

"The audience was so enamored with Lando, they could forgive Lando for anything," Billy Dee recalled. "If you're able to play a character that can be sort of a bad guy but has redeeming qualities, those are the best characters to play. That was a great challenge to me, to make him palatable, and it worked."

While fans, knowing the scope of Lando's role in the original *Star Wars* trilogy, are now less likely to berate Billy Dee in public, Billy Dee confessed that he thinks his role in *Jedi* could have gone even further. "I think if I had my way, I would have saved the day," he declared. "I thought that would have been the ultimate, because there's so many stories about Lando and his adventures."

Reminded that Lando did indeed help destroy the Death Star, Billy Dee said, "That meant a lot, but I guess I was looking to do the whole trip. If I had done the movie by myself I guess I would have been happy! I sort of forgot that the story is not about Lando and his hero-

a good feeling to be around people—that motivates me to smile."

Perhaps some of his elusive personality will come to light in his upcoming book. "It's an interesting way of presenting my life," Billy Dee said of the project, "because it's through my art but also through a lot of my ideas and thoughts, a lot of my thinking. Over the years, I would sit before a tape recorder and record my thoughts and my views on things, so a lot of the stuff is transcribed tapes."

Born in New York City in 1937, Billy Dee auditioned for his first role, in a Kurt Weill musical play, when he was 6, because "my mother was interested in introducing me to the acting world," he said, "so I have her to blame for all this!" He got the part, and on opening night, Billy Dee was sure he was a star.

"They had me walk across the stage two times," he remembered, "and then they said, 'Thank you very much, Billy.' I decided I didn't want to leave until I could walk across the stage a third time, and I embarrassed my mother so much because I started crying until they let me do it. I was a spoiled, precocious little boy who wanted his way and had always gotten his way.

"So they let me do it, and I think that's when it all hit me. I loved the idea of being on stage and being in front of an audience. It's very interesting when I think back on it, how things sort of just snapped right into place."

But it would be years until Billy Dee came close to acting again. Instead, he was an artist, a painter, attending Music and Art High School in New York. "Music and Art was a very special place," he recalled. "There was a very loose

didn't really take acting seriously. The director said to me, 'You've got a great deal of talent, but you should study.'"

Instead, he spent two years painting on scholarship at the National Academy of Design for the Fine Arts, only to be discovered yet again, this time by a casting director when Billy Dee accompanied a friend to an audition. Soon, Billy Dee was doing extra work with the likes of

Gavin McLeod (future captain of *The Love Boat*) and, finally, studying acting.

"It was a lot of training in those years," Billy Dee said. "You went from acting classes to fencing to dance—a whole system. In those days, it was sort of drummed into your head that you should spend two years studying before you get out and work, but I never adhered to that. I

Impossible soon followed, before he relocated to Los Angeles in 1970. "I had a little boy at the time," he said, "and I needed to make some money. I wanted to take my chances and see what I could do away from New York."

The gamble turned out to be just as successful as any wager laid by Lando Calrissian. Looking back on his Hollywood career, the actor

and *Mahogany* (1975), which was directed by Motown Records founder Berry Gordy—whom Billy Dee went on to portray in the 1992 TV miniseries *The Jacksons: An American Dream*. "It was his idea," Billy Dee said. "He always wanted to look like me. And I always said I only wanted to have his brains. It was fun. I really captured him pretty good as a matter of fact."

>> Clockwise from above: **Lando on Cloud City; Lando and Leia at Jabba's palace; piloting the *Millennium Falcon*; bidding farewell to Han Solo.**

thought if I ever get an opportunity, I'm going to take the opportunity."

Of course, opportunity knocked almost immediately, and soon Billy Dee was appearing on Broadway in plays like *The Cool World* and *A Taste of Honey*, and in his first film, *The Last Angry Man* (1959). A role on the daytime soap *Guiding Light*, and guest appearances on primetime series like *The FBI* and *Mission:*

said, "I've done a lot of films—some good, a lot of bad ones. There's one movie I did called *Giant Steps* (1992) which is, I think, one of the best roles I've ever done. It's about a jazz musician. I did that in Canada. And a movie I did called *Hit!* (1973) was sort of a revolutionary idea, for a black man to play a CIA agent. I headed up that cast."

The star teamed with Diana Ross in both *Lady Sings the Blues* (1972), his breakout role,

Billy Dee was also paired with comedy superstar Richard Pryor in three movies—*Lady Sings the Blues, Hit!,* and 1976's *The Bingo Long Traveling All-Stars & Motor Kings,* which also starred Billy Dee's *Star Wars* colleague James Earl Jones. "He was my pal," Billy Dee said of the man who would go on to lend his voice to Darth Vader. "He played my brother in the second play I did on Broadway, *The Cool World.*"

Through it all, Billy Dee became just as famous for his way with women as for his acting. "My mother used to talk about Rudolph Valentino a lot, and I always wanted to grow up to be like Valentino," he said. "Of course, I love the ladies, so when I did *Lady Sings the Blues*, I thought it was a great opportunity to display a kind of romanticism that people have never seen."

As a public service to our readers, the *Insider* pressed Billy Dee for the secrets of his approach to the ladies. "My mother says if I saw something attractive about anybody, I would have no compunction about saying anything about it," Billy Dee shared. "Maybe I just get away with it because I've somehow learned the art of charm—and it is an art. A lot of it has to do with self-awareness, how you perceive yourself. You're nice to people. You welcome people to you. You don't give of yourself for a long time, but you do it in a very pleasant way. Plus, you gotta be a little handsome too, I guess."

Immediately, he added, "You don't have to be handsome really, because there are guys who are very charming who are not handsome, but they're handsome inside. And you have to have a feeling of romance too. Romanticism is limitless. It includes swashbuckling, it includes duels, but it's all done with a certain flair. You don't take it all too seriously. It's not like you gotta have it."

It was that easy flair that catapulted Billy Dee to sex-symbol status. On one infamous episode of TV's *The Jeffersons*, wacky maid Florence (Marla Gibbs) was so overcome by guest star Billy Dee's presence that she fainted. "Women fainting, that was amazing to me," the star said, claiming that when women started passing out around him, "I didn't even have any fame at the time. It was happening all my life, actually. When I was three years old, I wandered off down the beach, and when my mother and father found me, I was surrounded by a bevy of ladies with cupid lips all over me. So I was pretty much destined for this life with the ladies."

Fulfilling that destiny has not been difficult, Billy Dee added. "I've always been a very good lover, and a friend."

Already a star, his fame reached an apex when *The Empire Strikes Back* was released in 1980. Billy Dee said being offered the part of

Lando Calrissian was the opportunity of a lifetime. "They called and I met with [director] Irv Kershner. We talked a lot about Eastern philosophy, which I was very much into, and he decided he wanted to work with me.

"I signed a two-picture deal with them," Billy Dee continued. "I was like everybody else—a fan. And then when it happened to me, I thought, 'Wow, this is great!' And then having dolls made of me was even better—effigies! I sign them all the time." The actor had been watching George Lucas' work for years. "I liked

>> From left to right: **Caped crusader! Billy D**ee poses in Lando's iconic cape; **A suave skiff! Billy D**ee on guard duty.

him ever since I saw *THX 1138* (1970) and I thought, 'Wow, what a unique movie, what a unique filmmaker!'"

Billy Dee remembered his "*Star Wars* experience" as a happy one. "Carrie [Fisher] and I became real good buddies," he said. "What I really enjoyed were the people that George embraced and gave work, the young people who were not necessarily in show business but were technically or scientifically trained. I would go over to where they were working and see what they were doing. They were brilliant, all young kids.

"See, I like young people," the father of two continued. "I love the energy, the ideas of young people. And I'm very supportive of young people, because when I was younger everybody supported me."

When he wasn't admiring the work of the

special-effects artists, Billy Dee could often be found wandering the enormous sets. "I was really quite impressed," he said. "It always amazed me, these guys who put all that stuff together, the artisans. I have always admired them. I was also quite impressed with the set that was created for Gotham City in *Batman*."

Billy Dee admits to some disappointment that he was overlooked in favor of Tommy Lee Jones when his *Batman* character, Harvey Dent, returned as a villain in *Batman Forever*. "I really wanted to play Harvey Dent when he became Two-Face," the actor said. "I really play good bad-guys. I love playing villains."

In fact, when the *Insider* talked to Billy Dee, he had just returned from shooting a Canadian film called *The Contract*, in which he plays a corrupt U.S. senator pursuing the presidency by any means necessary. Other post-Calrissian roles for Billy Dee have included two seasons (1984-86) as millionaire playboy Brady Lloyd on the hit TV soap *Dynasty* and one season (1992) as cowboy Aaron Grayson on *Lonesome Dove: The Series*.

And the actor has some casting ideas for who should play Lando's father (should such a role exist) in the new *Star Wars* prequel trilogy: "Me. I don't think any of those guys have what I have on screen. They don't understand it the way I understand it. They're good actors, but when it comes to a certain pedigree, we're miles apart."

Still, the actor's favorite role has remained the one he started with: artist. The painter had his first exhibition in Los Angeles in 1988, and is currently preparing for his latest showing, an exhibition of jazz-related works for a gallery in New Orleans. "Almost every evening, I paint, into the morning," Billy Dee revealed. "I've been painting and acting all my life. It's just a matter of using different materials. I'm never going to give up acting."

That's good news to his legions of fans, who know that wherever he appears, Billy Dee Williams will make his mark as indelibly as he did when he joined the *Star Wars* saga midstream to become one of its biggest and most beloved characters. "It's been the story of my career," Billy Dee reflected. "*Lady Sings the Blues*—same thing: that movie was Diana Ross' movie, but *I emerged* from that movie. I know that about myself." ☙

John Hollis
I, Lobot

A closer look at the characters that fleshed out the worlds o, Star Wars, and the talented actors who portrayed them

Try telling John Hollis how effective he was as Lobot, Lando Calrissian's cyborgian administrative aide in *The Empire Strikes Back*, and the veteran British actor responds with characteristic modesty. "If you've got a part," Hollis told the *Insider* "where you're walking around with lights flashing on your head, you can't really fail, can you?"

Perhaps, but while some actors might have been content to let the flashing lights do the acting for them, Hollis brought a stoic sense of purpose to Lobot that left an impression far more indelible than his memorable headgear. When Hollis subtly shifts his eyes toward Billy Dee Williams during one crucial Cloud City scene, he's not only indicating that Lando's plan to help the Rebels is underway, he's also signalling the audience that this mysterious new Calrissian character might not be so bad after all—and that there's more going on inside Lobot's head than just circuitry and wires.

"Originally, Lobot had quite a lot of lines to read," Hollis revealed. "But they had a discussion where they decided it would be better if he didn't talk, because he had been lobotomized, and he was getting messages through the computer. The dialogue was very much just answering questions put

to him by Billy Dee." Losing the lines, he said, "didn't bother me too much."

Hollis, 66, is just as unassuming when he describes his acting credits. "My film career has been very minimal, really," he insisted. "I've been more of a theatre, television and radio animal." But while Hollis has indeed appeared on over 150 British TV shows and recorded over 1500 radio

broadcasts for the BBC, his filmography, far from minimal, is about as, uh, maximal as one coul get.

In addition to the mighty *Empire*, Hollis genre credentials include the first two *Superman* movies and the 1980 *Flash Gordon* (in which he played a robotic minion of Ming the Merciless) as well as an episode of *Dr. Who* with Jon Pertwee as the Doctor. Quipped Hollis, "I barely worked on this planet."

In the first *Superman*, Hollis was a member of the Kryptonian Council of Elders—the huge billowy faces that angrily pronounce the evi General Zod, Non & Ursa, "Guilty!" He reprised the role in *Superman II*, when he popped out of a powerful crystal in the Man of Steel's Fortress of Soli tude and read the poem "Trees" by "Joyce Kilmer of the plane Earth." Hollis even played a Rus sian colonel in a scene that was cut out of *Superman IV· The Quest for Peace.* "I skipped *III*," Hollis la mented. "I don't know what happened!"

Even before donning his Lobotic headphones, Hollis was already a familiar face on British television. "I'm totally bald, so I've played a lot of villains," he said, on series such as *The Saint* and *The Avengers.* He started his career at England's Theatre Royale of Norwich in 1950

with fans thanks to the Kenner action figure of the character, which Hollis said he's got in his home in Twickenham, Middlesex, "hanging up in the kitchen on a hook—my wife says it's a good place for me to be."

In fact, it was the toy that gave the character his name, Hollis said, noting that in the original script, as well as in the final credits, he's just "Lando's Aide." But Hollis' strong performance and striking visual image (aided, of course, by conceptual artist Ralph McQuarrie and costume designer John Mollo) all but demanded an action figure of the character.

"When they did the marketing," the actor recalled, "they came up with the name Lobot, because he'd been lobotomized. I suppose 'Lando's Aide' wouldn't really mean anything."

Actually, that's doubtful, because by any name, John Hollis' character stands as one of the most surprisingly human—and memorable—of the *Star Wars* trilogy. With or without the flashing lights. ☮

"If you've got a part where you're walking around with lights flashing on your head, you can't really fail, can you?"

performing "Shakespeare and Chekov only. If you can do the classics," he said, "you can do everything, really."

But no amount of theatrical training could have prepared the actor for Lobot's unique challenge: acting with that heavy "brain-enhancing device" on his head. "That was murder," Hollis admitted. "It had to be self-contained—they didn't want any wires hanging out. So it was all battery-powered. They put it on a spring clip, so it clipped around my head. It was very heavy. At the end of the day, you were glad to get rid of it."

And there were many days; originally hired for just one week's work, Hollis ended up spending ten weeks on the Bespin set. "I remember the floor of Lando's world was absolutely white,

and no one was able to walk on it without cushions on," he recalled. "It was constantly being polished and mopped."

Much of his time at Elstree was spent acting alongside Billy Dee Williams. "He was a very cool character, a very laid-back man, very sophisticated, I thought," Hollis said. "He was very smart, and had a good sense of humor." That easy chemistry was crucial in making the Lando-Lobot relationship so natural onscreen, even without conversation.

But Hollis said dialogue wasn't the only thing Lobot had cut from *Empire*. "A lot of death scenes were filmed," he remembered. "There was a scene of me being carted off by men in white masks. But they would say, 'Oh, we might need you again. There were a lot of people getting arrested, but they were very wary about showing people die."

Though he was spared from death in the *Empire* editing room, Hollis nevertheless did not appear in *Return of the Jedi*. But Lobot lived on

Opposite page: John Hollis as he appears today, and Hollis as "Lando's aide", to be later named as Lobot, from The Empire Strikes Back. This page: Lobot in action.

VOTE **STAR WARS** ! DETAILS INSIDE!

BEST VILLAIN?

BEST HERO?

STAR WARS

AMAZING NEW
FICTION

RALPH
MCQUARRIE
REMEMBERED

ISSUE 134
JULY 2012
U.S. $7.99
Can $9.99

TITAN

STAR WARS THE **CLONE WARS** **SEASON 5 EXCLUSIVE!**

10 GREAT MOMENTS FROM SEASON 4

Episode titles revealed! New details teased!

BRIAN MUIR
DARTH VADER

ISSUE 134
JULY 2012

Star Wars: 123 released

Star Wars: ABC released

Knight Errant: Escape #2 released

Star Wars: Knights of the Old Republic Collection released

Darth Vader and the Ghost Prison #3 released

Star Wars: Lost Tribe of the Sith: The Collected Stories released

Blood Ties: Boba Fett is Dead #4 released

Darth Maul: Death Sentence #1 released

Were it not for the *Star Wars* information-hungry fanbase, many people involved in the franchise would go unsung. One such person is Brian Muir, a quiet and unassuming man who just happens to have sculpted Darth Vader's original helmet and armor. He even fashioned the Dark Lord's nose with his thumb!

It's a wonderful claim to fame, though Muir is not the type who courts fame. Instead, he is content in the knowledge that he played an important part in creating a motion picture icon.—**Jonathan Wilkins**

Brian Muir was born on April 15, 1952. The sculptor not only created the body armor for the first stormtroopers, the headpieces for several droids, and some finishing work on the C-3PO costume, he also sculpted Darth Vader's helmet and armor, based on concept art by Ralph McQuarrie.

MASTER CRAFTSMAN BRIAN MUIR IS THE MAN RESPONSIBLE FOR SCULPTING ONE OF CINEMA'S MOST ENDURING ICONS: DARTH VADER, AS WELL AS STORMTROOPER ARMOR, AND MORE BESIDES. HE TELLS *INSIDER* ABOUT HIS *STAR WARS* EXPERIENCE.
WORDS: MARK NEWBOLD & JAMES BURNS

Can you reveal something about yourself that will surprise *Star Wars* fans?
My first career choice when I was at school was to be a sports teacher. My primary passion was basketball and I was picked to play for my county. I then went for a trial for the England team. I played until injuries forced me to give up, but I then coached the National League youth teams until I was 50. I am now an enthusiastic follower of basketball from the comfort of my armchair.

What was your reaction to seeing *Star Wars* for the first time?
I, along with many crewmembers, had the opinion that the film was strange, and doubted it would be a huge success. It was only when I went to the cast and crew screening in London that I realized how wrong our opinions had been. After the opening sequence, when the Star Destroyer flies over the screen, the whole audience applauded. At the end of the screening, the crew showed their appreciation with a standing ovation. It was a real mark of respect as film crews are a hard bunch to impress!

Do you have a favorite scene?
It has to be the first sight of Darth Vader, when he emerges through the smoke on the Blockade Runner. To see his extraordinary presence on screen was incredible. It was the first time I had seen the character come to life.

How long did you work on *Star Wars*?
Initially, I was hired to do six weeks work on the film, but I ended up sculpting the stormtrooper armor, Darth Vader's mask, helmet, and armor, the heads of two droids: Death Star droid (below) and CZ-3 (right), and doing some work completing See-Threepio, which took over four months.

Do you have any *Star Wars* memorabilia?
I have an ever-expanding collection of all things *Star Wars*. I have a *Return of the Jedi* Vader mask and helmet, and a very accurate fan-made Stormtrooper helmet generously given to me. A unique addition to my collection is a pair of white clogs, embellished with the Imperial logo, which were presented to me by the Dutch Garrison of the 501st Legion.

What is your favorite *Star Wars* film?
It has to be *A New Hope*. Not only was it groundbreaking for its time, but it holds so many good memories for me. It was my first project back into the film industry after a break of three years. I had the pleasure of working with the great production designer John Barry, and the talented sculptress Liz Moore, and so many other skilled people who I still work with to this day. Without having been involved in the creation of Darth Vader and other characters in *A New Hope*, I would not now be having such a wonderful time traveling the world and meeting appreciative fans.

EXPANDED

Read more about Brian's work at
www.brianmuirvadersculptor.com

UNIVERSE

Mara Jade Comic Unveiled ▪ Terry Brooks to Write Novel Based on Episode I

STAR WARS®
INSIDER

Meet the kid who grew up to become

Darth
Vader

Photos from the
upcoming Star Wars film

An interview with
Doug Chiang, the man who
designs the new Star Wars

R2-D2 & Wicket
return for the prequels

An interview with prequel star
Jake Lloyd

ISSUE 39 U.S.A $4.50 CANADA $5.95

SHORT STORIES

KENNY BAKER AND WARWICK DAVIS

ISSUE 39
AUGUST/SEPTEMBER 1998

Tales of the Jedi: Redemption #2: The Search for Peace released

Vision of the Future released

Young Jedi Knights: Trouble on Cloud City released

Galaxy of Fear: The Hunger released

Tales of the Jedi: Redemption #3: Homecoming released

Starwars.com announces *The Phantom Menace* as the title of Episode I

Two of the best-loved characters in the saga, R2-D2 and Wicket, the gutsy Ewok warrior, are played by actors short on stature, but huge on personality: Kenny Baker and Warwick Davis.

This vintage interview, presented as a two-parter way back in *Insider* #39, sees the pair discussing their return to the saga as Episode I goes into production. Baker, of course, reprised his role as R2-D2, while Davis played three new characters—Wald, Weazel, and a Tatooine street trader—and even performed as Yoda.**—Jonathan Wilkins**

Kenneth George "Kenny" Baker was born on August 24, 1934, in Solihull near Birmingham in the UK. His career as an entertainer began in 1951 when he was invited to join a theatrical troupe. That led to a brief stint with the circus and a part in the first of many ice-skating shows. Around the same time, Baker formed a close friendship with his future Star Wars co-star Jack Purvis, and the pair developed the Mini-Tones stage act, which they performed together for many years. His film appearances include Circus of Horrors *(1960),* Flash Gordon *(1980),* Time Bandits *(1981),* Labyrinth *(1986), and* Willow *(1988). Baker passed away on August 13, 2016.*

Warwick Ashley Davis was born on February 3, 1970 in Epsom in the UK. When Davis was 11 years old, his grandmother heard a radio advertisement calling for people who were 1.2 meters tall or shorter to appear in the forthcoming Star Wars film, Return of the Jedi *(1983). Davis, who was born with Spondyloepiphyseal dysplasia congenita, a very rare form of dwarfism, applied, and ended up replacing a temporarily ill Kenny Baker as Wicket, the young Ewok who befriends Princess Leia and the rebels. The part led to a busy career including two spin-off Ewok movies, a starring role in the 1988 Lucasfilm blockbuster,* Willow, *and the TV comedy series* Life's Too Short *(2011—2013), with Ricky Gervais and Stephen Merchant.*

WHEN ARTOO MET WICKET

BY SCOTT CHERNOFF

STAR WARS LEGENDS **KENNY BAKER** (R2-D2) AND **WARWICK DAVIS** (WICKET THE EWOK) TELL THE *INSIDER* ABOUT RETURNING TO THE *STAR WARS* SAGA FOR EPISODE I

W arwick Davis and Kenny Baker have a lot in common, and it's more than just what meets the eye.

Both of the talented actors were hidden beneath elaborate costumes in the original *Star Wars* trilogy—in which Kenny played R2-D2 and Warwick was Wicket the Ewok—yet they made their characters two of the saga's most beloved. Both are British, and though neither of them ever set out to be actors, both of them are the world-famous stars of some of the most timeless and celebrated movies in cinematic history. (In addition to their *Star Wars* stints, Kenny starred in *Time Bandits* and also appeared in David Lynch's *The Elephant Man*, *Mona Lisa*, *Flash Gordon*, and the Oscar-winning *Amadeus*, while Warwick took the title role in George Lucas' fantasy epic *Willow*—'nuff said.)

As if all that wasn't enough, Warwick and Kenny are both returning for next year's *Star Wars: Episode I*, with Kenny reprising his legendary role as Artoo and Warwick coming through with no less than three new characters. And, yes, there's also the obvious trait these two actors share: both of them turned around expectations for little people by becoming giants of both the silver screen and the *Star Wars* universe.

As R2-D2—the fearless, inquisitive, do-gooding droid with a storied past—Baker projected his own zest for life with every one of

Artoo's trademark shakes and jiggles. With help from *Star Wars* sound designer Ben Burtt, as well as a remote-controlled Artoo used as a double for shots that required the robot to walk, fly through the air or perform other such stunts, Baker turned the little astromech droid into an unlikely Rebel hero.

Davis, meanwhile, made his *Star Wars* debut in *Return of the Jedi*, when his naturally enthusiastic and energetic performance as a background Ewok won him the plum role of Wicket, the trusting Ewok who befriends Princess Leia. Wicket became such a popular character that he was made the focal point of two Ewok TV-movies (released theatrically overseas) and the Saturday morning *Ewoks* cartoon.

Wicket's emergence as one of the trilogy's most popular characters was all the more amazing considering that the actor who played him had never before acted—indeed, he celebrated his 12th birthday on the *Jedi* set, having joined the production after his grandmother heard an ad on the radio looking for little people to be Ewoks. But since going on to star in *The Ewok Adventure: Caravan of Courage*, *Ewoks: The Battle for Endor* and *Willow*, as well as appearing in *Labyrinth* and now Episode I, Davis quickly became one of George Lucas' most prolific collaborators.

Now 28, Davis is also famous for playing the evil, madcap title character in all four *Leprechaun* movies—not to be confused with the recent

British production *A Very Unlucky Leprechaun*, in which he portrayed a nice Irish sprite. When he's not acting or playing dad with his infant daughter Annabelle and wife Samantha, Davis is helping other "short actors," with his Willow Management Company, which represents British performers no taller than five feet.

There was no such agency for Baker, 64, who got his show business start touring with an all-little-person revue, eventually hooking up with partner Jack Purvis. Together they formed the popular cabaret act, the Minitones. Film and television work soon followed for both, with careers skyrocketing when the two landed roles in the first *Star Wars* movie in 1976. (Purvis played the Chief Jawa, and went on to play the Chief Ugnaught in *The Empire Strikes Back* and the Ewok tribe leader Teebo in *Jedi*.)

Sadly, Purvis, who was paralyzed in a car accident in 1991, passed away last year (for more on Jack Purvis' life and career see *Insider* Issue 37). The death of his former partner capped a difficult period for Baker, who lost his wife of 26 years, Eileen, four years ago. But Baker, who is also the father of two sons and continues on with a solo cabaret act, retains an optimistic outlook on life, and told the *Insider* that he was happy to be returning to the *Star Wars* universe.

Recently, the *Insider* had the opportunity to catch up with both of these *Star Wars* stalwarts, 15 years after they teamed up in *Return of the Jedi*, and just a few months afer completing work on Episode I. **>>**

Illustration by Hugh Fleming

KENNY BAKER
ARTOO AND ME

HOW DID IT FEEL climbing back inside the R2-D2 costume for Episode I?

It was quite an event. I got to the studio early, before the film had started, to check out the robot. I found it was exactly the same robot, with the same old boots inside the feet. It had been used for other things since. Inside, there were one or two bits and pieces that weren't there when I was in it. We sorted it all out again and got it back to the shape it was in when I was inside it originally.

Did you play Artoo in anything else besides the *Star Wars* movies, like the Star Tours ride, "The Star Wars Holiday Special," TV commercials, or other personal appearances?

No, I did the three movies, the original three, and, didn't see the robot again until Episode I. I hadn't been inside it since *Jedi*.

Donning the old R2-D2 costume must have brought back a flood of memories.

It certainly did. We went to Tunisia, and we went to almost the same spot in the desert that we did the first one, and did quite a bit of shooting out there. It was pretty hôt, about 127 degrees on one day.

Is it even hotter inside Artoo? Do you have any kind of cooling system in there?

Everywhere is hot at those temperatures. I had a tiny fan, but that didn't do any good—it just moves the hot air around!

Can you see what's going on around you?

There's just an opaque window, about 4 inches at the most in diameter, and I couldn't see much at all. But I didn't need to, as long as I could see who I was supposed to be reacting to. I'm moving my head from one side to the other to follow the gist of the conversations. That was about it really. I didn't walk anywhere, because they used the three-legged remote-controlled robot to move around. My costume weighs about 80 pounds or something. It's quite heavy, and I couldn't physically move it, apart from wobbling and jeering around and moving the head.

A lot of personality comes through from your performance. What do you do inside Artoo to make the character your own?

I'm acting away inside this thing. You just have to act through the costume. You're still doing the facial expressions, and whatever you need to do, making noises, to try to give the character some life.

I've done that quite often over the years in different costumes. It's the way I move, I presume. That's what it must be. I've been told it's much more effective when I'm in R2-D2, as opposed to the remote-controlled robot. It's a robot, it doesn't really wobble and jiggle around, does it? Although it moves, it's kind of static in other respects. It's a natural movement of the robot that they want to see, and then that's coupled with the dialogue and with the sound effect, and eventually George gets what he wants.

It's hard to know what he does want at times, because you're doing what you're supposed to be doing and hoping it fits in with what's going on around you. You don't see much and you can't hear much, because of the

YOU JUST HAVE TO ACT THROUGH THE COSTUME. YOU'RE STILL DOING THE FACIAL EXPRESSIONS, AND WHATEVER YOU NEED TO DO, MAKING NOISES, TO TRY TO GIVE THE CHARACTER SOME LIFE

»THREE FOR THE ROAD Kenny Baker (left), Artoo, and *Insider* publisher Dan Madsen, all suited up for his background role, on the set of Episode I.

normous sound of the whirling of the lights nd stuff inside the head of the robot. There's uite a few electronics going on inside there, hich is fairly noisy.

s all that distracting?
Well, it doesn't help. You're slightly cut off from hat's going on around you. But it seems to work. It seems to come across OK eventually.

Did you ever worry that Artoo would be computer generated for the prequels?
It did cross my mind a few times— whether they were going to computerize the ob, or even get somebody else to do it. They could always find someone else, I suppose, if hey wanted to. But it happened they didn't, nd George came up and gave me a nice greeting when we met again t Leavesden studios, and everyone said they were pleased to see me again, so it was great.

They really did seem to be genuinely pleased hat I was with it. One of the first assistants said, "It's nice when you're on the

set, because it seems like *Star Wars* again." Just because I was there, it somehow gave the feeling to everybody that it was buzzing again. The atmosphere seemed to be just as electric as it once was.

Was there a lot of camaraderie on the set?
Oh, yeah. Ewan McGregor, Liam Neeson—we all had some good times together. I drank wine with Liam Neeson one night in Tunisia and got talking. Ewan McGregor's a nice, friendly guy, and I liked Natalie. She's a pretty girl, and I liked her mother, thought she was a very nice lady. Jake was great. I thought he was a lovely little

boy, as well as his family, his mother and father, and his sister.

There were a lot of nice people on the movie, and everyone's out there doing their best. Nobody argues. They're all in there to try and make a nice, happy movie, and there was nothing I could say was a bad experience at all. Everybody was enjoying themselves.

Who did you pal around with when you made the first trilogy?
Mark [Hamill] was good fun. He would come in with the boys and have a drink with everybody. Jack and I would take him out with us at night on the cabaret circuit in London, and show him what we did for our bread and butter. We used to take him with us sometimes when he felt like it, and he enjoyed it.

In *Return of the Jedi*, you also played Paploo. Was it fun taking on another role?
It wasn't fun at all, not in an Ewok suit! If you fell over, you couldn't get up again. You couldn't get in or out of your costume without a dresser, so if you did fall over in the woods, you would

had a few days off, we were sitting by the pool sunbathing, with little lizards flying around everywhere. We went up to the Grand Canyon from Yuma, one weekend when we weren't working. I also enjoyed California, in the redwoods [where the Ewok scenes were filmed], apart from the costumes.

Was Star Wars your first movie?

No, I did *Circus of Horrors* and another film in England, and television films. *Star Wars* was just another film, as far as we were concerned at the time. It was nothing special. Nobody expected it to be something terrific. I thought if Alec Guinness was in it, it must have some credibility. He must know more than I do!

But nobody thought it was going to be any good. They all thought, 'What a load of rub-

Labyrinth and *The Dark Crystal*, as well as *Willow* for George.

Jack and I eventually moved and lived close to each other in North London, which is near Elstree and Leavesden. It was all happening in that area. We were married and had wives and kids and were working every day and every night. We were doing one-nighters all over the place, getting up at 7 with the kids, then going to do a commercial, then doing two shows the same night and then coming home at 2 o'clock in the morning.

And it went on and on until we wanted a night off. But Jack said, "Don't bother, keep working. It won't last forever." Which was true enough. It didn't last.

This was the first Star Wars you did without Jack. Did his absence affect your experience?

It did. They had these creatures walking around where all you could see was the costume and the little legs underneath it, and it reminded me of Jack, this guy inside this square box with just little legs underneath it, funny-looking thing.

Poor old Jack. He died last year in October just after the movie. I used to go to see him a lot in the lunch breaks. He only lived just down the street, so I used to have my lunch with him in the garden, and it was great to see him. He was stuck in this wheelchair paralyzed, but we'd gotten used to it over the years. Then he died one Tuesday morning. He just didn't feel very well and was practically dead before they got him into the hospital.

The trouble is, the older you get, the more these sort of things happen. There's nothing you can do about it. You just have to go on with life and keep going. That's what I've been doing anyway. ☉

[THE EWOKS] WERE CUTE, GREAT LITTLE CHARACTERS. THEY WERE LOVELY, BUT TO WORK IN THEM, UNBELIEVABLE.

just have to lay there until someone discovered you. Plus, you had rubber all around you and you were sweating and you couldn't see where you were going. It was very, very uncomfortable, but we did it because we wanted to make the movie a success.

Those costumes were just unbelievable because you had pajamas on, then you had the foam rubber, then you had the fur, skin, then you had the belt and the armory and several bows and arrows, and the headdress, and you had the gloves on, and then you had the feet on. It was all foam rubber and fur. Within five minutes you were boiling over with the heat. You couldn't breathe, you couldn't see where you were going. Very uncomfortable. They were cute, great little characters. They were lovely, but to work in them, unbelievable. I wouldn't be an Ewok again, I don't think, even if they asked me to be.

Which Star Wars movie was the most fun to make?

I enjoyed working [on *Jedi*] in Yuma, Arizona, on the big sail barge in the desert there. That was nice, and we stayed at a nice motel, and I used to play the harmonica with the band at night when we came back to the hotel. I'd play the harmonica, and dance—we were dancing with Carrie Fisher! And we were by a pool. If we

bish is this?' You couldn't understand it at first. It was very confusing—Obi-Wan Kenobi and all these weird, funny names that you'd never heard of before, which at the time were really hard to get your tongue around. The kids got them quickly, but as usual the adults thought, 'What the heck's all this about?'

How did you get into performing?

Well, I fell into it, really. I was going to be a commercial artist. I'd left school, and I just met somebody in the street and went on tour with this midget review! The show was in town, and I met this person and she was near the theater. I said, "I'm going to see the show tonight," and she said, "Would you like to join the show?"

She said to go and see the owner of the show, and he asked, "What can you do?" I said, "Well I can ride a bike, I can whistle, I can roller skate," and he said, "Welcome to the show." I traveled for about three years with the show. That was in 1950. I didn't meet Jack until 1960, when I got into the ice show at Wembley and we did *Snow White*, and *Peter Pan* on ice.

That's how we got the double act. We were the Minitones, a vaudeville act. We would do cabaret and pantomime and whatever else came our way—television, sketches with comedians on weekly shows. We also did a few things for Jim Henson before he died—

WARWICK DAVIS
KICK IT WITH WICKET

SO LET ME GET THIS STRAIGHT—you play *three* characters in Episode I?

Yes, more or less. My main character is called Wald. He's best friend to Anakin Skywalker. He's a masked character. But another character I did, I'm a spectator at an event, and I spent the whole day at Leavesden basically sitting in bleachers and moving my head left to right. You'll recognize me as that other character (photo on opposite page) because I only have hair extensions. I'm also watching the scene as Wald, so I'm in the same place twice!

The third role I did was very brief. I was standing there and lingering, and George just said, "Go and get on a costume." I ran into

YOU HAVE TO ASK YOURSELF HOW CAN I USE MY BODY TO MAKE THIS MOOD COME ACROSS?

make-up and said, "Make me look different." So they made me very dirty and seedy and George said, "All right, that'll do, walk behind the main characters." So you'll see me sneaking through.

Will you be performing the voice of Wald yourself?

I'm not sure what they're doing. I was speaking the dialogue under the mask. For *Jedi*, I understand it was an American Indian woman who did my voice. For this one, who knows? Maybe James Earl Jones will do my voice!

Was returning to *Star Wars* kind of like returning to your childhood?

Yes, it was. The Episode I first assistant director Chris Newman, was known as the Ewok wrangler on *Jedi*, because he was responsible for coordinating all of the Ewoks. It was really great.

What was it like filming in Tunisia?

It was thrilling for me. The routine of filming out there—our calls each day in Tunisia were 4 a.m., because they wanted to avoid the heat. It was like a military operation every morning, everybody marching out to their jeeps in total silence, and then we're driven off through the desert.

It was just getting light when we got to our location about 45 minutes later. As soon as the sun came up over the horizon, you would immediately feel the heat. You haven't even got a shadow—the sun is that high. That's why I think George loves to go there—because it looks like a different world.

The set they built in the desert—Mos Espa—the things that stood out for me were the moisture vaporators. That was *Star Wars* for me. I was standing in the middle of a three-dimensional *Star Wars*. Some people trekked off to try and find the old sets. They were looking for the rock where Ben Kenobi sat. I think they found it. I don't think rocks like that move. Actually we filmed in a little area called Tataouine. I think that's where George got the idea [for Tatooine].

What is Wald like?

The character is kind of similar to Wicket, being a young character, I think that inquisitiveness of looking at R2-D2 was my own personality coming through in Wicket, and I tried to recreate that with Wald.

Is it difficult to convey those nuances through a mask?

It's a different approach. You don't have your eyes or mouth. You have to ask yourself, 'How can I use my body to make this mood come

across?' I started with this walk. I just observed. I thought, what would I pick up on if I was six years old. There is thought that goes in—you can't just throw on a head and stand around there.

How do you deal with the heat inside the costume, especially out in the desert?

In everything you do with a head or where you're enclosed, you're going to get steamy—your own personal sauna. But how it affects you is all in your mind. You just have to chill out with it.

When you first played Wicket, you were 11 years old. What did you think of young Jake Lloyd, with whom you share most of your scenes in the prequel?

He was great. An older actor would have

push them for their abilities. We represent over 80 actors, and our only criterion is you must be five feet or under. Basically, all we ask for is enthusiasm. I think that's the most important thing in this business.

We had two people in *Star Wars*. One of our clients, Michaela Cottrell, played a Jedi Councilor, and Ray Griffiths was the stand-in for Jake Lloyd, and he played "Gonk" [also known as Power Droid]. Officially, he was filmed for a reference scene for a CG character. He was involved in the whole shoot.

Getting that phone call from [casting director] Robin Gurland, I'll never forget—"George would love to talk to you about playing a new character and I'd love to talk to you about Willow Management and using some of your actors!" I think I probably had the same enthusiasm now that I did back then [for *Jedi*]. It was an honor and a privilige. I was thrilled to get that call.

Have you gotten any calls about Episodes II and III?

I don't know yet. I've made suggestions for characters I could play. I told [casting director] Robin Gurland I'd love to play a baddie! That would be fun. ☻

---

collapsed under the pressure, but every line, he had right. You never had to re-shoot it because Jake didn't get it right. A very nice boy.

Was there as much excitement on the set this time around as there was for *Jedi*?

From my point of view, more excitement, because the *Special Editions* had just come out, so there was a feeling that we were really working on something special. I went to the *Star Wars Special Edition* premiere in London. It was fantastic to sit there in the cinema and watch it again.

Warwick, let's face it: some fans claim that the Ewoks are too cute to be in the *Star Wars* saga. As the cutest Ewok of them all, please set these misguided souls straight.

Well, I can see it from both sides of the coin, but I kind of like Ewoks. I wouldn't be right where I am now if George hadn't thought of Ewoks! But I just like the concept—these little, primitive, peace-loving creatures overthrowing this technologically advanced and totally evil Empire. I think they're fun, and kids love them. The fans have got *The Empire Strikes Back* if they want to get all dark and moody.

Are you still interested in directing?

After *Jedi*, I got really into directing. I bought a video camera and started making home videos, won some competitions. Then I started

taking it seriously, and it became a lot less fun! But I did bring my camera to Tunisia and filmed the drive across the desert.

Tell me about Willow Personal Management.

I started it four years ago with my father-in-law, Peter Burroughs. I have an agent, ICM, in London, but by and large there really wasn't any proper representation for short actors in London. They weren't treated as actors—it was just, "We need some dwarves for these shows."

We try to be more personal with it. We

I JUST LIKE THE CONCEPT— THESE LITTLE, PRIMITIVE, PEACE-LOVING CREATURES OVERTHROWING THIS TECHNOLOGICALLY ADVANCED AND TOTALLY EVIL EMPIRE.

BACK TO THE FRONTLINES IN *STAR WARS*: BATTLEFRONT II

STAR WARS
INSIDER

ISSUE 85

VADER IS BORN

REVENGE OF THE SITH ON DVD
SEE IT AGAIN FOR THE FIRST TIME

EXCLUSIVE!
VADER FICTION

WHO'S WHO
IN THE DELEGATION OF 2000

POSTERS OF EPISODE V
RARELY SEEN IMAGES FROM
THE EMPIRE STRIKES BACK

FICTION • BOOKS • COMICS • TOYS • GAMING • FANDOM • MOVIES • COLLECTIBLES • SHOP

DISPLAY UNTIL FEB. 6, 2006
January/February 2006
U.S. $6.99/Canada $9.49

AN IDG COMMUNICATIONS PUBLICATION

EXCLUSIVE ONLINE CONTENT!
• THE IRON CHEF OF FILMMAKING • *STAR WARS* WEB-
STRIPS • GALACTIC GALLERY: NEVER-SEEN-BEFORE ART

BANTHA TRACKS
• DROID DOME CAPS
• *STAR WARS* ENVELOPE ART

starwars.com

THE MAGAZINE OF HYPERSPACE: THE OFFICIAL STAR WARS FAN CLUB

THE EMPIRE STRIKES BACK
POSTER ART

ISSUE 85
JAN/FEB 2006

Republic #81 released

Knights of the Old Republic #1: *Commencement, Part 1* released

Outbound Flight released

Phil Brown (Owen Lars) dies

Star Wars: Empire at War released

Knights of the Old Republic #2: *Commencement, Part 2* released

Empire #40: *The Wrong Side of the War, Part 5* released

Republic Commando: Triple Zero released

Star Wars Miniatures: Attack on Endor released

Each film in the original *Star Wars* trilogy featured a diverse array of poster art by some of the leading artists of the day. Noted illustrators such as the Brothers Hildebrandt, Tom Jung, Drew Struzan, and Tom Chantrell all contributed their vision of the saga, creating posters that are still instantly recognizable as their work today.

The art for *The Empire Strikes Back* is particularly evocative, from Tom Jung's poster featuring Darth Vader striding dramatically across a montage depicting the action from the movie, to Roger Kastel's iconic *Gone with the Wind*-style take, depicting Han and Leia in a romantic clinch.

Pete Vilmur, a *Star Wars* historian of the highest order, takes an in-depth look at these and other posters for *Empire*, some very familiar, others rarely seen.—**Jonathan Wilkins**

OF EPISODE V:
THE EMPIRE STRIKES BACK

By Pete Vilmur

WHILE the Lucasfilm Image Archives is able to provide some early poster concepts for *A New Hope*, the actual sketches and photographs that chronicled the development of the campaign's familiar posters—the Style "C" and "D," for example—are few and far between. Fortunately, this is not the case with *The Empire Strikes Back*.

A fair amount of concept material was available for co-author Steve Sansweet and me (*The Star Wars Poster Book*) to track the evolution of the three major U.S. posters for the saga's first sequel—the 1979 Advance, the 1980 "Gone with the Wind" Style "A," and the Tom Jung Style "B." Occasionally, we found the final designs had even been influenced by other artists' concepts—Lawrence Noble's unused "outreaching Vader" clearly is related to Tom Jung's final Style "B" composition.

It also became apparent that the art director was interested in capitalizing on the success of Jung's original *Star Wars* Style "A" image as many variations on that theme were conceived as potential *Empire* contenders. Looking back, this approach seems totally misguided, but you can't blame them for trying to match the transcendent effect of Jung's original. Marketers were quick to learn that *Empire* was a different film than *A New Hope* and that the posters needed to reflect that.

In addition to Jung, a couple other *New Hope* veterans were invited back to submit concepts for *Empire*. Tom Chantrell created a lavish design that placed Luke at the center of the action, just like he'd done for his famous *Star Wars* Style "C" poster. Artist Noriyoshi Ohrai, whose sprawling 1978 gatefold artwork captured the hardware aesthetic of *A New Hope* for a Japanese movie magazine, offered several different compositions with one eventually landing the posters for several international campaigns.

Of course, the Archives contain a fair share of tangent concepts as well, primarily from anonymous artists. These provide fascinating insights into the marketing strategies behind what many consider the original trilogy's finest chapter. It's amazing how so many different ideas could be distilled into three or four key poster images.

EMPIRE 1979 ADVANCE

The singular image of Darth Vader, whose return was a given for the 1980 summer sequel to *Star Wars*, fronted the *Empire* campaign on the first Advance posters (opposite page) sent out to theaters during the 1979 holiday season. Ad agency Seiniger and Associates hired photographer Bob Peak Jr., son of the famous movie poster illustrator, to shoot the Dark Lord's portrait for the poster. As revealed in this pair of photographs from the Image Archives, the image of Vader's helmet was actually flipped for the final poster itself.

"GONE WITH THE WIND" STYLE "A"

Early on, Lucas insisted that he wanted an *Empire* poster image that captured the spirit of an epic romance, à la *Gone with the Wind*. Senior Vice President/ Marketing Sid Ganis took the order to heart, contracting several different artists to take a swing at the Han/ Leia swoon. Ironically, the artist who designed the famous image for the 1967 re-release of the 1939 Civil War epic, Tom Jung, was not selected to do an *Empire* incarnation. That task fell to artist Roger Kastel.

From Kastel's early sketches (below left), it's interesting to note the absence of some characters—Boba Fett and Chewbacca—while others were included— bounty hunter IG-88 and Lando Calrissian. Cloud City was also depicted and made it to the first color comp (above left) along with a more full-figured Princess Leia. Boba Fett, the more obvious choice to fill the bounty hunter role in the image, replaced IG-88.

The painting evolved to include more of Luke's tauntaun and less of Leia's figure, while adding the X-wing fighters (opposite page, above left). At this stage, the artwork was photographed and used for several publishing applications, such as the novel's cover and soundtrack album.

The dimensions of the artwork, which fell short of the traditional one-sheet's 1:1.5 ratio, were probably inspired by those used on the *A New Hope* posters, which included a large white field in the lower quarter for the credit block. Because it was decided that the artwork should fill the entire poster this time, the painting was extended at the tope and bottom, creating a discernible horizontal seam where the extensions were added (opposite page, below left). These are commonly mistaken by cautious collectors as the photographed fold lines of a bootleg poster, which they are not.

For the final release poster (opposite page, right), the composition was pared down and the warmer tones were cooled a bit. The removal of the Lando Calrissian character from the image prompted an inquiry from the actor's agent, accelerating the release of the campaign's third poster, the Style "B."

THE STAR WARS SAGA CONTINUES

THE EMPIRE STRIKES BACK

TOM JUNG STRIKES BACK

Some of the earliest concepts for *Empire* appear to be by artist Tom Jung and were clearly inspired by his famous *Star Wars* Style "A" poster. Probably solicited at the art director's request, these include a triumphant Vader with lightsaber (seen on opposite page, bottom right), a *Star Wars* half-sheet-like image of Luke and Leia before Vader (above), and a rather silly depiction of Luke in full Hoth gear joined by a scantily clad Leia side-saddling his tauntaun (right). Clearly, these didn't deliver the desired effect.

Jung was ultimately able to capture the film's adventurous spirit in artwork that graced the campaign's second release, or Style "B" poster (opposite page, left). The poster's cool hues also suggested the film's darker tone with Vader tenaciously dominating the composition. His outstretched hand became the signature feature of this and two re-release posters spawned by *Empire* inspired in part by an unused concept submitted by artist Lawrence Noble (opposite page, right).

Although Noble's concept was not chosen for the print campaign, it was used on a limited professional advertisement in 1980 and was picked up 10 years later by Kilian Enterprises for use as an *Empire* anniversary poster.

A long time ago in a galaxy far far away...

STAR WARS

NORIYOSHI OHRAI

Japan's Noriyoshi Ohrai, a prolific illustrator who is well known for a series of stunning *Godzilla* re-release posters in Japan, produced numerous works for the *Star Wars* saga that stretch back to 1978. On the strength of a *Star Wars* illustration he had published in a Japanese movie magazine, Ohrai was asked to submit a number of concepts for the *Empire* poster campaign. His comps were aesthetically varied with different elements and color schemes assigned to each. One, which featured the *Millennium Falcon* front and center (above center), was re-imagined two years later for a Japanese-dubbed commemorative poster of *A New Hope*.

The *Falcon* was ultimately featured in Ohrai's final *Empire* illustration (right), which incorporated elements from several of his concepts and settled on a green and violet color scheme. A favorite of many fans, this artwork was used in several international markets, including Australia.

OTHER CONCEPTS

Thomas Chantrell, well known to fans for his stunning *Star Wars* Style "C" poster image, turned in a highly polished illustration for *Empire* as well, this time featuring the warm tones of a Bespin sunset (right). Luke once again dominates the composition as he did in the artist's Style "C" version.

This unattributed concept (below left), which incorporates many of Ralph McQuarrie's preproduction paintings for *Empire*, was probably considered for the British quad release. McQuarrie's stylized Darth Vader graphic at the center was used extensively for production and promotional purposes in England.

Illustrators closely associated with the *Conan the Barbarian* book series were favored by *Star Wars* marketers in the early days—Frank Frazetta was approached for *A New Hope* but had prior commitments that prevented him from submitting a concept. Boris Vallejo was called on for *Empire* and created a wonderful set of Burger King and theatrical premium posters. Artist Sanjulián was also asked to provide a poster sketch as evidenced by this signed illustration found in the Archives (opposite page, lower left).

This unattributed concept (below right) features Vader and Luke locked in combat with Leia looking on. Though it doesn't deliver the formal illustrative style that fans have come to expect from a *Star Wars* poster, it achieves a certain storybook feel with its strong composition and impressionistic style.

STAR WARS
INSIDER®

ISSUE #157
U.S. $7.99
CAN $9.99
MAY/JUNE 2015

TITAN

MILLENNIUM FALCON

A SPACESHIP FIT FOR KIDS

ISSUE 157

MAY/JUNE 2015

Back in the late 1970s/early 1980s, Kenner's *Millennium Falcon* playset was the toy that every child wanted. I remember dropping outrageous hints to my parents that I'd quite like this beautifully realized replica of Han Solo's cooler-than-cool ship for my birthday. Sure enough, when the day came it was there. I felt like the luckiest boy alive.

Some years later I actually met Mark Boudreaux, the man who designed the iconic toy that means so much to me and countless other kids. I've been lucky enough to meet some big names from the *Star Wars* saga, but in this case I couldn't help but gush my appreciation at the many happy memories his work had afforded me!—**Jonathan Wilkins**

THE FASTEST HUNK OF JUNK IN THE TOYBOX!

WORDS: NEIL EDWARDS 🔱 ||||||||||||||||||||

Star Wars creator George Lucas was one of the first people in the film industry to truly foresee the huge potential of movie merchandising to connect with young audiences. This was best demonstrated by the astounding success of the original Kenner line of action figures and vehicles, with one of the most important toys surely being Han Solo's famed smuggling freighter, the *Millennium Falcon*.

The *Millennium Falcon* has to be one of the most iconic vehicles in screen history. Just shown its silhouette, we'd wager even most non-*Star Wars* fans would be able to identify the fastest hunk of junk in the galaxy, such is its fame within pop culture. Given its popularity, we're not the only ones who woke up thrilled one birthday or Christmas morning to find a big, gift-wrapped box containing our very own *Falcon*.

While some changes had to be made in the *Falcon*'s journey from the screen to toy shelves— the scaled-down cockpit of the toy could seat only two, unlike the four-seat cockpit of the movies—the resulting toy was still a remarkably true representation of the ship we know and love. Looking back, what's surprising is just how much detail from *A New Hope*

was included, from the secret smuggling compartments to the Dejarik table, to the training remote. The *Falcon* toy provided many hours of gameplay for countless young fans thanks to its myriad features, enabling them to re-enact the movies or to imagine their own further adventures for the ship and its crew.

One of the added benefits of the toy was that thanks to its large size, interior space and many features, it also functioned as a playset or even as a carrier for your action figures (possibly inspiring later toys, like

1982's Rebel Transport, to be partly designed with that very purpose in mind). As with the *Star Wars* universe, the possibilities were endless.

The *Falcon* toy became a mainstay of the *Star Wars* toy range, through *The Empire Strikes Back* and *Return of the Jedi*. While the packaging may have changed to reflect each movie, the toy remained the same. Other representations of the ship have since reached toy shelves, too, made by the likes of Hasbro or LEGO, continuing the

Falcon's play appeal for successive generations of fans. One thing's for sure, though—this baby's got a few surprises left in her!

WHAT THEY SAID

"They said, 'Hey, Mark, you want to work on this big vehicle?' I said, 'Sure.' We thought that *Star Wars* was pretty cool, but it didn't have the 30 years of history we have now."—**Mark Boudreaux**, *Millennium Falcon* toy designer, *Star Wars Insider* #106, January 2009

ESSENTIAL TRIVIA

In 1986, a freight-loading external rover, or F-LER (a small one-man ship for transferring smaller cargoes) for the *Millennium Falcon* was designed for a Kenner toyline called "The Epic Continues." The craft was designed to fit between the forward mandibles of the *Falcon*. That line was canceled, with the F-LER eventually appeared in the *Millennium Falcon Owner's Workshop Manual* published by Del Rey and Haynes in 2012. A similar small craft, the YT-XC, which fitted behind the *Falcon*'s docking ring, was included with the Hasbro Legacy Collection *Millennium Falcon* in 2009. As designer Mark Boudreaux joked to *Star Wars Insider*, "It was always there; you just never saw it in the films." 🔱

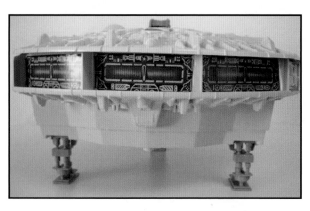